Worldwide Accl
No More Lies Ab

D1462317

"The One Million Dollar Book!"

—USA Today

"Unputdownable!"

—New York Post

"Witty."

—Boston Globe

"Skilfully written, intricately woven and meticulously executed."

—BBC

"Comes out punching ... delivers all the jabs, upper cuts, left-hooks and the final knockdown for the count out. Read it!"

—Washington Post

"Entertaining, rich in language and articulate."

—New York Times

"Powerfully delivered."

—Time

"Deals a heavy blow to the misconceptions about Africa."

—Book Review

"In *No More Lies About Africa* Chief Nangoli's language is forceful and highly captivating."

—Ogot Benge, Weekly Topic
(Uganda)

"One cannot but laud Chief Nangoli's book for its unabashed defence of the African personality."

—*Wahome Mutahi,*
Nation, **(Kenya)**

"Chief Nangoli writes the way African books should be written."

—*Catherine Githeru,*
Nation, **(Kenya)**

"*No More Lies About Africa* is a spirited attempt to rebut European lies about Africa."

—*Prof. William Ochieng*
Kenyan Historian

"Informative."

—*Felister Magabe,*
Business Times, **(Tanzania)**

"Chief Nangoli's Book, is important in demolishing the white man's misconceptions of the black man."

—*Donald Woods,*
author of **'Biko'** *and*
'Asking For Trouble.'

"Penetrating insights into Africa."

—*Today*

"Deeply moving ... unarguably the most constructive book out of Africa."

—*Sunday Telegraph*

"Chief Nangoli knows how to put his sentences together."

—*Concord*

"This book is a load of rubbish!"

—*Canadian missionary*
working in Kenya

"I missed my flight at JFK Airport while perusing this book."

—*Reader from New York*

"When I'm down, I read *No More Lies About Africa* to recharge my batteries."

—*Hous ewife*
from New Jersey

"This book should be read by every African in the world."

—*Reader from Ghana*

"*No More Lies About Africa* is a thriller. I couldn't put it down."

—*Dr. Jennette Cascone,*
History professor,
USA

"A classic."

—*IHT*

"Exhilarating, fast moving— it is a knockout!"

—*The Daily Gleaner,*
Jamaica

Also by the same author:

- ROLIHLAHLA MANDELA & APARTHEID

- THE AFRICAN CAUSE — *I Speak to Mother Africa*

- NO MORE LIES ABOUT AFRICA — *Here is the truth From an African*

- LORDS OF SLAVERY — *The Case for Reparation to Africa*

- THE CHIEF'S GUIDE TO ORGANIC LOVE & RELATIONSHIPS

- HOW AFRICANS LIVED & ACHIEVED CIVILIZATION BEFORE EUROPEANS CAME   (TV documentary)

Books in preparation

- THE CHIEF'S ENGLISH DIARIES —*Uncovers Sizzling Revelations about the English*

- I AM PREPARED TO DIE — *The Trial and Imprisonment of Chief Rolihlahla Mandela*

- MARCUS GARVEY
  The African Hope (film)

- GLIMPSE INTO THE WHITE SOUL — *The story of a young African who travels to the white man's land and discovers himself*

- THE GOLDEN STOOL — *The Story of African Peoples*

No More Lies About Africa

Orders and Enquiries

Email: nambozo@eudoramail.com

No More Lies About Africa.
Copyright © 2002 by C. M. N. Productions
Copyright © 1987 by Chief Musamaali Nangoli
Originally published in the USA by A.H. Publishers
First Edition published 1987
Reprinted 1987 (twice)
Reprinted 1988 (twice)
Reprinted 1990 (three times)
Reprinted 1991 (four times)
Reprinted 1992 (four times)
Reprinted 1994 (four times)

1. African History   2. African Culture   3.African Politics/Current Affairs
4. Economics

ISBN: 0 940385-03-1 (Paper back)

SECOND EDITION 2002 Africa

No More Lies About Africa

Here is the Truth from an African

CHIEF MUSAMAALI NANGOLI

SECOND   EDITION

Publishers

This book is dedicated to Amy Jacques Garvey and Miriam Makeba—two great African mothers. And in loving memory of Wadada Musani, for whom plenty was yet to come.

Contents

4.   Captivity and Colonialism:

Part Two: MARCUS MOZIAH GARVEY:

Acknowledgements

Without the following people, this book could never have been written:

All the storytellers across Africa, too many to mention by name, educated me in African history and culture.

Chief Musamaali and Mugide, my maternal grandparents; your input into what I know about Africa, is priceless.

Gugga Elukana Wakadala; your lessons to me in African religion, came in handy.

Gugga William Gidagui; wanyala naabi majesi gesi wapezaga. Umusakulu Alozio Mafabi; wanyala kusomesa kubikale bya Africa. Baba Maserejje; you taught me the art of thought. Senje Esereda Maserejje; you taught me the art of discipline. Kuku Janet Manafa, wanyala kusomesa zisambo. Kuku wo Wazikonya, wanyala kusomesa kulinda inyanga.

Geoff and Beth Ballard, your kindness to me knew no bounds. David and Barbara Rees, you were incredible in Paris!

Jan Harlan; without your practical support, mobility would have been impossible. Also your faith in me has been an ocean of encouragement. Maria Harlan; that you opened the doors of your beautiful home and so charmingly entertained me, restored my faith in humanity again. Delores Jones; you showed me the true African spirit in America. Danny Stacher: your kindness and help to me cannot adequately be put in words.

Dr. Maria Schantz: thank you for welcoming me to the US!

Thank you for being there for me when I needed you most.

Gugga Busima Nangoli; your unshaken belief in me over the years, has enabled me to write books such as this one. Thank you for being my number one fan!

Brother Makau Mulumba; your enthusiasm for this book was so huge that it re-charged and re-activated my batteries so that I could go on writing—asante sana ndugu!

Mukwasu Wangolo; utyo aso-wanyala byosi. Ikwisamu lugosi. Mukodomi Bertulumayo Mukasa; thank you for your belief in me.

Mzee Ali Hassan (Ruksa) Mwinyi; I will for ever be grateful to you for your boundless kindness to me.

Dr. Salmin Amour; I have benefited from your intellectual gifts and thank you for your warmth and brotherly love.

Dr. John Henrik Clarke; your keen eye saw the faults of the manuscript in draft form.

Dr. Jennette Cascone; your excitement about the book, was all I needed for re-assurance. Your editing couldn't be bettered.

Dr. Marcus Garvey Jr., and Dr. Julius Garvey; thank you for sharing wonderful memories of your father with me. That you endorsed so strongly my approach to your great father, really encouraged me.

Simon Booker of Ebony Magazine and Daniel Mathews of African Bibliographic Center showed me the way in America.

G.J. Brown, my father-in-law; I know I have not paid bride price for your beautiful daughter. One of these days I'm going to surprise you. Thank you for allowing me 'free' board so that I could write. That red snapper fish you used to cook really made the words flow!

Brother Chinua Achebe; your belief in the book and faith in my abilities was a lake of encouragement. Christopher Bunoti; as ever, you are a source of encouragement and support.

My long suffering wife, Nambozo; what can I say? Your beauty, is a constant reminder to me that I'm a lucky man. Your help with the book, gave it the shape it didn't have. Your being there, gave me a sense of stability a man needs! Writers are not the easiest of people to live with. Their moods change with every chapter or book they write. When they are down and unable to write, they conveniently take it out on their wives—you bore all that crap with the kind of dignity very few women can match! My son, Mandela; thank you for not complaining whenever I had to throw you out of my study so that I could write.

As ever, I am particularly grateful to Nicholas and Meresi Nangoli, my parents; who were always my source of knowledge and inspiration—Mwanyala kuba basaali balayi, Mayi ni Baba. Were Alinde!

I acknowledge with thanks Collins Publishers' permission to quote from *The African Child* by Camara Laye. Also Ben Mugimba's photo under polygamy.

The omissions and the shortcomings of the book however, are entirely my inescapable responsibility.

Part One

AFRICAN HISTORY

1
Prologue

Hello, My Dear Reader!

M y full names are Chief Musamaali Busima Gidagui Nawodya Nangoli. I was born in Uganda many, *many* years ago. Don't ask me how old I am. All I know is that I was born under a mango tree, one rainy day during coffee season and while circumcision ceremonies were going on. I possess neither a birth certificate nor a document to that effect. Tell me what records are kept under a mango tree! Like every Mugisu boy, I had to face the knife (circumcision). So when I was eleven coffee seasons old, I demanded the knife. The elders obliged—the knife came. The surgeon descended upon me and cut and cut and *cut!* I was as silent as a rock. This single act immediately buried my youth and I became a man in the eyes of my people.

As a young handsome boy growing up in Africa under the feet of my elders, I was always curious as to how my people lived before the white man came. I am reliably informed by those who knew me that as a boy, I was extremely intelligent, apart from being the most handsome boy in my village, and those beyond (according to most young girls.) The gap between my upper-front teeth, simply drove them crazy!

I used to ask many questions. When I grew older, I was taken to a missionary school to be 'educated.' There, I found out that I had been *discovered* by the white man, that my ways were primitive, that I had to become a Christian, and that I had to be baptized. I was given the white man's name, Peter. I was told that the God my people had worshipped for centuries was the wrong God and that I had to wear the white man's clothes as mine were primitive. I was taught the white man's languages and his ways and told to despise my own. All this would take place at school. Then I would go home to my village to talk to my grandfather, Chief Musamaali. He would tell me about the days before the white man came—about the great empires, kingdoms with kings and queens, and how my people used to worship God, cared for their own, cultivated the land, buried the dead, and so on. He told me how he as a young man would walk 'tall' among his people. How when he spoke, the whole of his village, and all those surrounding, would listen. How he kept all his six wives happy! And now how the white man had come and thrown his weight about as if he possessed three testicles. How the white man had attempted to strip him of his respect and dignity among his people. I would listen to all this.

Back at school, I would be told that the white man, as a Christian, loved his neighbour and didn't hate!

So one day, I climbed the white man's flying machine he calls aeroplane and went and *went,* until I reached Britain, the *mother* country. Upon arrival, I duly presented the whole of myself to the Immigration Department at Gatwick Airport. Behind the check-in desk stood a short plump dude of about forty. He wore a funeral expression on his face and probably couldn't remember the last time he smiled. With guard on, he went into attack.

"Passport, please!"

"I don't have one."

"You don't what?"

"No passport!"

"And why not, may I ask?"

"This is my home!" I said, pointing to the earth.

"Which one?" The white man wanted to know.

"The whole of Great Britain. Besides, your own fore-fathers didn't have passports when they went to Africa, did they?" I hit back.

The white man carefully looked me over momentarily destabilized, as he wondered as to which mental asylum I had just escaped from in Africa.

"And which idiot misguided you into such an expensive lie about Britain being *your* home."

"A white man like you—in Uganda," I replied.

"He lied to you!"

"But a white man, especially an English man, *never* lies!"

"That's a bloody lie! What's your name?"

"Peter," I proudly announced.

"What?"

"Pete!" I diligently removed the 'r' to sound more English.

"What the bloody hell are you doing with a white man's name?"

"It's my Christian name, sir!"

"Your Christian—what?"

"Christian name."

"Who lied to you?"

"Another white man like you, in Uganda."

"Boy, you're a real bleeding mess!"

"OK!" I said, "Since the whole of me has arrived, why don't I become your visitor—like we do in Africa?"

"Certainly not!" He shot back.

"Why not?"

"We're already over-crowded as it is." The white man was by now red in the face.

"But I'm entitled to be here. I'm a man. I am an equal human being like you."

"Human being—perhaps. Equal, no!"

"You say 'am not equal to you?"

"Certainly not!"

"How many testicles do you possess to prove your superiority over me?" I asked purposely to provoke him as I no longer cared. My fate had already been decided. I was not getting into Britain.

"Look old chap, I am not here to answer your silly questions." He hit back.

"So what are you going to do with me now that I'm here?" I inquired.

"Send you right back to whatever jungles you came from."

"But surely, officer, that is bad manners," I pleaded.

"Here, it bloody isn't, mate."

So I was promptly rounded up and thrown out of *mother* country—Britain.

Years later, I was able to get into Britain. One bright Sunday morning, soon after my arrival, I went to the white man's church to pray to God.

St. James' Church in Muswell Hill, North London, was a Church of England affiliate or a Protestant church as we called it in Uganda. The congregation was all white. Upon entering, I looked around for space on the pews and saw one with four worshippers on it—three men and one woman. All whites. As I approached it, I whispered, "Good morning," to them and settled down. Clad a in three-piece suit I had recently acquired and with a parting in my hair, I felt myself every bit an English gentleman. How I felt a sense of belonging! How I felt I had arrived! How I had practiced the colonial English accent and was ready to unleash it on whoever cared to talk to me. Every evening, how I would stand in front of a mirror, push my nose up narrowing the nostrils, and speak as if

I had a bad cold. That way, I would sound as close to an English man as possible. I would go: "Ahaa u know, ma name ahaa is Pete, a-ndaah 'am fro ... Ugaandah, u know!" I went over these lines several times until I felt I had mastered the English accent. I had also diligently practiced putting on white people's plastic grin.

Suddenly, one by one, my fellow worshippers jumped off the bench and looked for seats elsewhere. As more and more worshippers piled into the church, I noticed they all carefully avoided my bench. A cold chill descended upon me, but quickly gave way to sweat of embarrassment. Surely, I couldn't be stinking as I had showered that morning and doused myself with cologne. Besides, I am a stickler for cleanliness.

How I felt lonely in a building full of human beings! How I wished I had been born white! How I missed Africa at the same time! At the end of the service, the Reverend came up to me. He was a tall, lean, statuesque man of about fifty, with pencil-line lips.

"What is your name?"

"Gudu morning, sir," I answered.

"Morning! What is your name?"

"Pete."

"Where do you come from?"

"I am fro ... ahaa Ugaandah, u know."

"What on earth are you doing here?"

"I am hiyaah to ahaa pray to God!"

"No, no, no! I mean what brings you to the UK?"

"Oh, heavens above! 'Am hiyaah to ahaaa study law, u know!"

"I see! You know, young man, I have nothing personally against you, but it's the parishioners. They don't want a coloured man in this church."

"Oh, thank goodness for that, Reverend, because I'm not ahaa coloured, u know!"

"What then are you?"

"I am ahaa Christian, u know."

"That may well be, but you can't worship here. Here's where you should go."

He proceeded to scribble an address on a piece of paper, handed it to me and, believe it or not, wished me a *pleasant* stay in the UK. As I left St. James' Church, completely dejected, (and bloody pissed off) I couldn't help wondering what life was going to be like* in a country where even Reverends were bigots!

The following Sunday, I went to the address in Nottinghill. It was a Baptist Church. Inside, the congregation was all black.

Therefore, as a young man growing up, I was torn between what I was being taught at school and the stories my grandfather related to me. Added to this, what I experienced first hand as I travelled through the white man's land. I was thoroughly confused and angry. Very angry! The anger I talk about manifests itself in the pages that follow.

This is by way of telling you, Dear Reader, what led to the research and writing of this book. I travelled the breadths, the lengths and widths of Africa researching into our past for over ten years. I spoke to hundreds of elders and story-tellers across Africa, and for hours, they would tell me about our ways and past. This is how this book was researched not through one single library!

No More Lies About Africa is a deliberate title for this book because the lies about Africa, are deliberate. If ever there was one thing that all African peoples the world over agree on, it's the fact that Europeans told, and continue to tell wicked lies about the continent of Africa for diabolic purposes.

Now is the time to set the record straight. These lies, if allowed to continue unchallenged, will forever do irreparable damage to the image of Africa and her peoples.

It is not so much that these lies are *lies,* but the fact that they have a stigma attached to them and are passed on from generation to generation.

Time is long due, for peoples of Africa and African descent to proudly look at Africa, as a land with a revered past and draw inspiration from that past, as the basis for the present and hope for the future. I deeply felt that it was incumbent upon me as a son of Africa, to seek to set the record straight. To expect otherwise, was to continue dreaming without mitigation. For this, I offer no apologies! If this book in any way serves the purpose of setting the record straight, then there lies my reward!

2
African History

THE LIES AND TRUTHS

A lot of nonsense and wicked lies about Africa, have been written by the so-called Western 'experts' on African history. Usually one or two trips to the continent, and a general chat with a few brainwashed Africans, has overnight turned these Western scholars into authorities on the history and affairs of the continent.

In these 'great' works on Africa, one never fails to come across misleading declarations such as: this European **discovered** this and that; another European was the **first** man to see the Zambezi or Ruwenzori. These are things which already existed and had African names. The naked fact that Africans had seen these rivers, mountains, lakes, and oceans before the European invasion, or indeed had discovered them themselves, fails to occur to these 'experts' on Africa!

THE LIES

That until the first white man set foot on African soil,
the African was without a culture of his own;
 Was without religion, hence did not know God;
Was without science and technology;
Was without education, hence could not read or write;
Was without shelter, hence put up in trees and lived
by hunting and employing primitive methods to trap
his kill. *Poppy Cock!*

Given that the educational system in Africa is predomi-
nantly influenced by the West, this kind of material
inevitably finds its way into schools where the African is
'educated!' Bombarded with one *fact* after another, carefully detailing the failures and inadequacies of his ancestors, the African inevitably grows to despise his self-
image, past and culture.

Tragically, until now, there have not been enough
written materials by Africans on Africa, to straighten the
record. Or the few that there are, have been by retrogres-
sive Africans serving the interest of their masters who
are the exploiters of Africa.

Indeed, as Marcus Garvey warned, "The history of
African people would have to be written by themselves
if the truth had to be told." He, perhaps, did not budget
for the apologetics and homeguards.

Lakes and mountains already existed and had African names—
Europeans lied to the whole world that they had discovered them

King Sobhuza II of Swiziland. Africans knew the art of government
before Europeans came

MARCUS GARVEY

In order to understand Marcus Garvey and what he set out to achieve for the African peoples of the world, one must look deeply into the history of Africa, the original home of all humankind, and more recently, the origin of all black peoples outside Africa.

As we will see later, Marcus Garvey was what he was because of what he knew of the true history of the African people. After all, he knew that his forefathers had once lived proudly as kings with kingdoms, emperors with empires, and chiefs with chieftains; had governed themselves; cultivated their land; grown coffee, tea, fruits, bananas, potatoes, had therefore fed themselves; clothed themselves; and given birth to the earliest and greatest civilizations on earth. And yet, these proud kingdoms, empires with wealth and all other civilizations had been invaded, looted and destroyed. He was aware that his forefathers were captured and taken to foreign lands and their land colonized and subjected to ruthless foreign rule by these invaders.

As we will find out in the fourth chapter, it were the horrors of captivity and the arrogance of colonialism, which first inspired Garvey in the early part of the century, to set out on the tough and lonely course of trying to redeem all African peoples. A people who once walked free, manned their own affairs, but later were enslaved and in many ways are still in bondage and chains.

WHY AFRICAN HISTORY?

Firstly, because there is such a thing as African History. Secondly, African peoples all over the world need to be properly educated about Africa's glorious past. That past has been at best, misunderstood, and at worst, taken out of context.

I have called this the history of the African people deliberately, in order to embrace all the African peoples of the world wherever they may be. No history of the African people is complete unless that history begins with Africa. The mere fact that African people live in the Americas, the West Indies and Europe, having first been chained and taken against their will to strange lands as **captives**, doesn't, in my opinion, remove their link with Mother Africa.

> All blacks, therefore, are Africans, I submit

Their roots are still deeply entrenched in Africa, the land of their forefathers.

The discovery by Alex Haley of his *Roots* in the Gambia, bears the strongest evidence for this contention. It has done a lot to enhance the feeling of **belonging** to Africa by most sons and daughters who are descendants of former captives. It has (I hope) above everything else, given them a sense of belonging somewhere.

But what of their history and that of ours, Africans still living in Africa?

MORE LIES

No history of humankind has been as distorted as that of Africa and the Africans. A good job has been done in trying to convince Africans living in the diaspora that their 'true' history started with the ships which carried them into captivity and servitude.

The truth of the matter is they are still part and parcel of the history of the continent that for centuries was the home of their forefathers. The fact that they have adapted and acquired a different way of life in their imposed surround ings does not alter that gospel truth. Regretfully, to this day, these brothers and sisters still suffer from, among other things, a lack of identity and acceptance in their new societies.

It is nearly two hundred years since the likes of William Wilberforce and organizations, such as the Quakers, successfully campaigned for the total abolition of human trade. But tragically, even two centuries later, the legacy of captivity still lingers on in these, their new settlements.

Re-emancipation* has not entirely removed the scars of captivity in their minds, (sons and daughters of former captives), any more than it has removed the attitude of 'captive master' and a sense of superiority in the minds of sons and daughters of former **captive owners.**

It leaves the field wide open for argument, whether it

*RE-EMANCIPATION, *because African Peoples were already emancipated before they were taken captive or colonized.*

King Mutesa II of Buganda, Unganda

Africans cultivated their land—grew coffee, fruits and vegetables

was humanly conceivable that African peoples after the ordeal of being taken as captives, and with the stigma of captivity around their necks, would recover adequately after re-emancipation, to feel full human beings again. It is also debatable, as to whether white peoples would recover from human trade enough so as not to lapse into fantasies of 'superior race.'

As we'll see later, Garvey was as optimistic about the prospects of African peoples total re-emancipation and acceptance by white peoples in their society, as he was of the latter's ability to do so.

*   *   *

Africa, was for generations, presented to the outside world by her ruthless invaders as the 'dark continent,' inhabited by savages, intellectually lacking, un-Christian and morally uncivilized. Hence, the Africans outside Africa, could hardly be blamed for not wanting to be reminded of, or associated with, Mother Africa. The story of the 'history' of their forefathers was more than they could stomach!

Strange as it may sound, it was not until recently, barely twenty years, that the truth about the history of Africa started to emerge. Scholars of African history with the aid of eminent archaeologists such as Dr. Luis Leakey, started approaching African history more cautiously and objectively.

Dr. Leakey, working in East Africa, has unearthed a lot of evidence to suggest that not only was there civilization and culture in Africa before her invasion by Europeans, but also that Africa is the home of the earliest man and the world. The great nineteenth century scientist, Charles Darwin, was also of this view amid great criticism from fellow scientists. Great attention, has been given by contemporary historians to the great empires and kingdoms that flourished in Africa long before Europeans knew the art   of administration.

And yet, strong as this evidence is, there still remains considerable doubts in the minds of many both inside and outside Africa as to its authenticity. Later, I'll examine in greater detail the doubts and objection to these claims. But now I will concern myself with the true history of the continent and the myths that have led to its distortion.

*   *   *

For a long time, the African was presented by the Europeans as they saw him. He was judged not by his own standards, but by those foreign to him. He was told that he had been 'discovered' and hence rescued from total obscurity. He was persuaded to believe that the color of his skin was 'inferior' to that of his victors and that his environment proved he was a 'half-baked species!' That his culture and traditions were 'primitive' and that he had to adapt to new 'civilized' ways if he was to catch up with the rest of the world.

Vanquished in his own land, the African had very few alternatives but to believe these lies. This was after captivity and on the eve of colonialism.

In fairness, very little was known about our glorious past by the invaders. Regrettably though, the distortion was

The world famous pyramids—built without mortor, cement or American aid

The Great Zimbabwe Palace, also built without British aid

sinister as the horrors of captivity and the arrogance of colonialism were later to demonstrate.

> The distorted picture and the lies about Africa suited human trade handsomely and justified colonialism magnificently in the eyes of the invading Europeans

EVIDENCE OF AFRICA'S GLORIOUS PAST

Therefore, a critical examination of Africa before any invasion is imperative as it does not only paint a different picture, but also enables the continent to be judged on merit with the aid of the evidence that has come to light so far. The next chapter deals in more details with how Africans lived before contact with the outside world.

Africa, as the findings of archaeologists and historians tell us, was the home of the first man to walk the earth. The remains of men found in East Africa are several million years older than the ones dug up in Europe or anywhere else! Some of the evidence that has given archaeologists clues about early life are human bones, tools, weapons, rock paintings, the art of writing, and other signs of life—adding to the sheer intelligence and ability of early man in exploiting the environment in which he found himself. Also unearthed are medals, coins, plus uniquely carved images in bronze of kings, queens, emperors, and images of animals, such as horses and camels giving clues as to the early kingdoms' wealth and forms of travel.

African craft

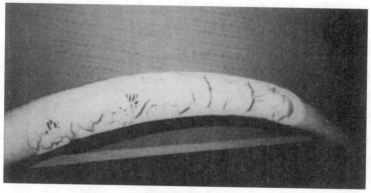

Ivory carving

I'll examine concrete examples of civilization and development in Africa before her contact with the outside world. But before I do so, special tribute has to be paid to ancient Egypt. Why Egypt? For the simple reason that it was there that civilization as we know it today, was born hundreds of thousands of years ago.

There were attempts by some Western scholars, wanting further to discredit the Sub-Sahara Africa and to disassociate Egypt with all her glorious history and culture from the rest of Africa. There is another claim that Egyptians were not of African origin, and therefore, they were not Africans. This unfortunate view, though still being held by Africa's exploiters, has been discredited. Ask any Egyptian whether he/she is African or Arab and the proud reply will be: "African of course!" This I confirmed on several trips there.

It is true that the European civilization is largely built on the achievements of the ancient Greeks. But the ancient Greeks in turn built their civilization following in the footsteps of the ancient Egyptians. This is what I mean by Africa was the birthplace of the earliest and greatest civilization on earth!

Such discoveries, as writing, painting, carving, drawing, mining, farming, building, and numerous ways of surviving by man in his natural environment were first made on the continent of Africa. They were discovered by Africans, experimented and practised by them long before one single white man had set foot in Africa.

The Africans had also established trade routes which were unequalled at the time any where else in the world. Gold was the most basic trading commodity. Coins up in Europe are mainly made from gold mined in Africa. It was through trade that Africans had their first encounter with people from the outside world. Great trading cities such as Timbuktu in Mali, were the center of most of the gold trade and other commodities, such as salt and spice.

The great Empires and kingdoms of Ghana, Mali, Songhai, and Kanem-Bornu controlled most of the trade and the trade routes.

It is said that Mansa Musa, one of the greatest rulers of the Kingdom of Mali, was so rich in gold that when he made a pilgrimage to Mecca in 1324, determined to show the outside world his wealth, carried gold with him to give away. He stopped over in Egypt and gave away so much gold there that the Egyptian currency almost lost value! Most of the gold traders at the time were the Mandinka people, who mined it as well.

Of all these empires, the Ghana Empire was the earliest founded around the second century A.D. It came to be known as the Gold Coast, symbolizing its wealth in gold, until Kwame Nkrumah renamed it Ghana on regaining independence in 1957. The Mali Empire was certainly the strongest of them as Mansa Musa set upon expanding it.

It was not only in West Africa where such development had taken place, but as the Portuguese, led by Vasco da Gama, were to find out on arrival to East Africa, the

Africans there were just as advanced and versatile.

Much later, the great thief Cecil Rhodes, found in Central and Southern Africa such degree of development and advancement that it is said he could hardly believe African men were behind it! Such arrogance and idiocy!

Happily, there still stands remnants of monuments which are a clear testimony to the advancement of the African, long before white men set foot on African soil. The Great Zimbabwe Palace in Zimbabwe, the world-famous pyramids in Egypt, and the forts on the East African coast of Mombasa are notable examples. And all were built without American aid! Also many sculptures, paintings, writings, for example: The Hieroglyphics, (ancient form of writing) and carvings grace many museums all over the world.

But that is not all. There is also evidence of great scholars, scientists, teachers, doctors, as well as spiritual leaders during this epoch of pre-European invasion. Africa has also produced no less than three popes in her neglected history! The architecture of this time was so advanced that both the pyramids and the Great Zimbabwe Palace were built without mortar or cement! How about that for architectural ingenuity?

African Religion

Then the monstrous lie that Africans did not know God!
The truth is the Africans recognized the power of God.
They may not have congregated together every Sunday
led into prayer by some Bishop, nonetheless, they worshipped in their own way which was uniquely African.

> The joke then (albeit real one) is, when the white man
> came to Africa, he had the Bible in his hands. Today,
> the African has The Bible in his hands, and the white
> man has the land!

So much for missionary work in Africa!
Let us now go back and find out the **truth** about how
Africans lived before Europeans came to **improve** things.

3

How Africans Lived
&
Achieved Civilization Before Europeans Came

Africa was never a 'dark' continent before the arrival of Europeans any more than Europe was a 'dark' continent before African men and women went there. Africa was as unknown to the West, as the West was unknown to Africa. To conclude therefore that, only that which Europeans knew little or nothing about had to be 'dark' and un-civilized, constituted ignorance and arrogance of the highest order!

Almost every known work on African history has failed to address this crucial point. The very fact that Africa as a continent did exist before contact with the outside world bears the strongest evidence to challenge this myth.

Africa was never without the magnificence of her sunshine—
therefore could never have been 'dark'

An African never smiles or laughs unless it comes from the bottom
of his heart

> At no time in recorded memory was Africa lost,
> therefore, Africa couldn't have been found
> or discovered!

At no time was Africa without the magnificence of her sunshine—so Africa couldn't have been 'dark.' If some European traveller arrived on the shores of Africa during the night and left before sunrise, and then went on to write that Africa was always dark, then whoever believed the bastard, swallowed a bitter lie and nothing else.

At no time was Africa without the wonder of her rivers, lakes, mountains, vegetation, minerals, rich soils for farming, game for hunting, crops, and fruits, so she couldn't have been the unhabitable place that books by Western scholars tell us it was. For people to have lived there in the first place the conditions had to be livable.

At no time was Africa without the uniqueness of her culture, languages, customs, technology, and forms of dress, so civilization must have occurred there long before.

At no time was Africa without the beauty of her populace living there, reproducing, and caring for their own as did other people.

At no time were Africans searching for other lands beyond Africa because they were dissatisfied with their own.

Indeed, at no time was the African eager to depart from Africa, as the fierce resistance to being taken captive by Europeans later in the seventeenth century, demonstrated. The African was proudly African, content to be so, and aspired to be nothing else!

Even the most avid critics of Africa's past are yet to produce evidence that shows that when the first batch of Europeans set foot on African soil, they found an indolent people starving and slaughtering each other for power, possessions, and influence as were the cases in the First and Second European Wars,* last century.

The irony of this great mythology about the 'dark' continent, is that the same Europeans who propagated it found it necessary to recommend further adventures in Africa, to their governments back in Europe. Not only did further adventures by Europeans take place in Africa, but the Europeans found Africa so hospitable as to come to stay. Europeans still live in Africa to this day!

The great nineteenth century thief, Cecil Rhodes, was dying from some mysterious disease in Europe. Cancer, I believe. Modern medication known to Europeans at the time, had been tried with little success. It turned out that the adverse weather conditions in Europe were aggra-

---

*EUROPEAN WARS *as opposed to* WORLD WARS, *because both Wars were started by and ultimately benefited Europe. Until now, even though African Peoples gave their lives for democracy in these Wars, they have been denied the fruits of that democracy.*

vating his condition. Africa, with her warm habitable climate and medicine, was suggested as an alternative for the dying Rhodes. To Africa's ever lasting sorrow and regret, the African weather conditions and medicine performed miracles on Rhodes and he lived. Infact, he lived long enough to have robbed southern Africa clean. This, in spite of the fact that the African healers who treated him refused to take a fee for their efforts, to show Rhodes Africa's hospitality and generosity.

Rhodes was not the only European who enjoyed African hospitality. Henry Stanley, David Livingstone, Lugard, and Vasco da Gama are other notable examples of Europeans who, in spite of themselves, were made welcome by unsuspecting Africans who treated them as visitors.

> It mattered little to the African that these men had arrived uninvited and were total strangers. They were sick, the Africans treated them free of charge; they were thirsty, the Africans gave them water to drink; they were hungry, the Africans gave them food to eat; and they were homeless, the Africans gave them shelter!

In return for this boundless hospitality and generosity, the African was stabbed in the back, robbed of his land—his women kidnapped and raped by these men who went around posing as missionaries and explorers. Men whose intentions were anything but honourable. Men who were up to no good and out to line their pockets as subsequent events in Africa showed. Men whose real purpose for coming to Africa, was to prepare the continent for Europe's eventual take over, and exploitation. Who can seriously deny that?

Why then, should I, as an African, find cause to trust the white man? The white man who through the years has lied to me, robbed me, tortured me and killed me. The white man, who to this day, occupies my land and tells me to go jump in the sea! The white man who has abused my hospitality. The white man, who above all, constantly urinates on any efforts by me to live with him as an equal in my land!

I have turned the other cheek, and I have now run out of cheeks to turn!

So reader, please take note before I go further into *How Africans lived before Europeans arrived.* At no time was Africa lost; at no time was Africa dark; at no time was Africa without civilization, and most importantly, at no time were Africans without their revered culture, the remnants of which happily survive to this day.

Let us now look closely at some aspects of African culture, and I swear in the revered names of Masaba and Kilimanjaro, that this is the absolute truth and nothing but the whole truth, from me, Son of Africa. From now on, if you hear or read anything different, please disregard it.

AFRICAN CULTURE

In accordance with the very best of our traditions, I welcome you to African culture! I hope that after enduring me to the end, you will be better educated about African culture and past.

Our culture, has been around as long as African peoples have been. That is a long, long time! Of course as years have gone by, evolutionary changes within the culture, have taken place. Some habits, once practised by past generations, have either been modified, changed, or abandoned altogether by succeeding generations. But the main body of African culture—those very things which distinguish them from peoples elsewhere, remain intact—thank heavens!

Perhaps the only time that the African and his culture nearly parted company, was with influences from without. Tragically, these influences were not only about conquest and domination, they were also about the attempt to kill African culture.

As evidenced by the goings on in present day Africa, these outside influences have succeeded in contaminating, hence diluting this rich culture. There is tragically the tendency in Africa, in her quest for so-called modernization, to run away from this rich culture.

The culture, is therefore in danger of being extinct. On the continent of Africa today, one is reminded more of the legacy of colonialism, and less of the survival of the African culture. I don't know about you, but for me, as an African, this really turns my stomach around!

WHAT EXACTLY IS CULTURE?

Before we go any further, let us understand what culture is. Culture is a language or languages people speak, the way they behave, live, relate to one another, dress, worship their God, care for their own, marry for reproductive purposes, name or baptize their children, regard their children, treat the elderly, bury their dead, and generally, the way that they carry on—a way that distinguishes them from other peoples of the world. Just as we talk of Chinese culture, European culture Asian culture, in this context, we talk of African culture—no one culture superior to the other.

Admittedly, some practices within certain cultures appear **odd** and unusual to peoples from without. But that's because those practices are observed from the point of view of **another** culture. But observed from the context of that particular ethos, they are not at all odd.

That was the mistake our European *visitors* made on the eve of their arrival in Africa. They judged Africa by standards foreign to Africa. They looked at Africa from the point of view of Europe. What habits they didn't understand, they labelled primitive and set upon destroying them. No other continent in the world has had this dubious distinction of having another culture imposed upon it, as was the case with Africa vis-a-vis Europe.

Present day problems that confront the continent of

Africa are directly attributed to this injection of a foreign culture.

Moral force propelled by one's culture inevitably begets uncapped allegiance to one's own race and country.

The African today is neither loyal to his race nor country. But has instead, strong loyalties to himself as an individual and to foreign interests. Years of imported cultural values from without, have destroyed his **Africaness** and replaced it with a distorted personality that is neither African nor European. He intellectually best expresses himself through foreign mediums and interprets his affairs via Western paradigms. Like a fish out of water, he has no choice but to perish sooner than later!

Since the African and European cultures are diametrically opposed to one another, attempts to merge them or to have them co-exist, have produced lamentable problems for Africa. Instead of existing side by side, the Western culture has tended to despise the African culture. Old habits die hard! Diluted though the African culture is as a result of Western intervention, it remains ingrained in every African born and bred in or outside Africa. Consequently, the African today finds himself with the dilemma of holding on to what has been his for centuries, and that which has been imposed upon him and promises heaven on earth. More often that not, hell has been delivered instead. Proving once more that one may succeed in changing the way people think but not that which they are about. That 's the power of a culture. You can tamper with it, but you can't destroy it. **You can take a man from Africa but you can't take Africa out of the man!** In a nutshell then, the African culture happily survives to this day in spite of attempts to destroy it.

The same languages that African peoples spoke before Europeans arrived are still spoken today. As we will see later in the chapter, many habits Africans practiced for centuries before are still alive and well in Africa today, e.g., the naming of new born babies, regard for the elderly, marriage, worship of god, dress, and a host of other customs.

These practices, however, are exclusively confined to rural Africa. So-called urban Africa is relentless in its efforts to kill African culture. One prays that the great and powerful spirit of Masaba*[1] the revered, will cast a magic spell upon these Wazungu Africans*[2] to stop them from destroying our culture!

ANCIENT AFRICAN   SOCIETY

Once upon a time in Africa, we paid no taxes, there was no crime, there was no police, there was no inflation, there was no unemployment, men did not beat or divorce their wives, then the white man came to improve things!

*[1] *Masaba is believed to be the original father of most of Bantu speaking Africans who make up 80% of Africans.*
*[2] *In Kiswahili it refers to Africans who have completely adopted European ways and actually look down upon African ways.*

The good old days! Tragically, those days are gone. Perhaps their magic never to be recaptured again—at least not in the immediate future!

Those were the days of the Golden Stool. Those were the days when Africa stood as a towering giant with men and women of affairs and purpose.

> Those were the days when Africa belonged to Africans

Those were the days of proud kings, emperors and chiefs ruling over flourishing kingdoms and empires! Those were the days. The ancient African societies then were highly organized and sophisticated.

Each kingdom or empire was governed by laws that were for all intent and purposes, products of African culture. Each law embraced every aspect of the African culture and was reinforced according to the custom of that kingdom or empire.

Emphasis was placed on rehabilitation of offenders and forgiving those whose shortcomings resulted from genuine need. For example: if a man 'nationalized' a neighbour's chicken and could establish genuine need, then there was no case to answer! Persistence of the habit however, would result into being 'sentenced' to replace the chickens.

Respect for the elders (those who saw the sun first) was paramount.

The rulers at the time were for practical purposes dictators but the benevolent kind. Their power, though

absolute, had nontheless to reflect the wishes of their subjects. Sharing was an aspect of African culture that was
stressed at every level of society. No one ate unless all could
eat. The needs of the individual were the needs of the
society as a whole. Offense by an individual against another
individual was considered an offense against the entire
society. It was the duty of every member of society to see
to it that the welfare of everybody was taken care of.

Inter-marriage was encouraged in order to strengthen
the ties between individual kingdoms. Every parent in
society was a **parent** to all the children in that society
and hence was charged with the responsibility of discipline.
Individualism and selfishness were discouraged and scor-
ned. Everything was done for the good of all.

The old African society was therefore governed by
strong traditions and customs. Crime was despised and the
need for it reduced. Land and property, were regarded as
belonging to all humanity and bestowed upon humanity
by the good grace of God. That everything man owned,
ultimately belonged to God (who gives and takes away)
therefore, to steal or damage property was regarded as an
act of offending God.

Man was the extension of God on earth, so the Africans
believed. Harm to fellow man constituted harm to God,
The Creator.

The woman was God's gift to man and earth, and on her
shoulders, God placed the responsibility of reproduction
and continuity. This belief is still widely held in many

parts of Africa.

ASPECTS OF ANCIENT AFRICAN CIVILIZATION

Africa in her meridian splendor, invented the arts of writing, building, music, communication, methods of travel, and painting. Africa, therefore, is responsible for six of the greatest civilizations known to humankind—no small achievement by any standard.

Tragically though, credit for these inventions, has been wrongly given to ancient Greece. Ancient Greece was doing what Africans had done centuries before. Not one single piece of history found in Greece is older than pre-historic monuments and various pieces unearthed in Africa. Not a single one!

The ancient Greeks in their quest for knowledge travelled across the Mediterranean Sea into North Africa and there, to their *amazement*, we are told, encountered wonders of buildings, crafts and paintings, as they had never seen before. These travellers enrolled in schools of learning, in thought, building, and survival methods by man in his environment. Many of them attended the University of Timbuktu in Mali, West Africa. This university is reput to be one of the oldest places of learning in the world.

Students of ancient history today widely acknowledge that Africa was the original home of man on earth. Alongside his bones was found tools he used for hunting for food, rock paintings, and weapons for survival.

As of today, there's hardly a single culture in the entire world that hasn't got in it some aspects of Africa's ancient civilization. They may not acknowledge it, but that's human nature.

Of all the civilizations achieved by Africans, none surpass those that demand respect and care for the elderly. These are aspects of African culture deep-rooted in the African.

CHARACTERISTICS OF AN AFRICAN

Basically, the African is like all other human beings. He breathes in and out. He has his good days and bad days. He has feelings and feels physical pain no less. He bleeds red blood. He loves and hates.

In those basic biological terms, believe it or not, the African is like everybody else. Where he differs is in his unique character. His strong cultural upbringing makes him notoriously people oriented and gregarious. He is highly sensitive, emotional, and excitable.

The African **never** smiles or laughs unless it is from the bottom of the heart. He abhors hypocrisy and is totally unimpressed by material wealth as the criterion for judging a person's character. A person is as good or as bad as his heart. Africans believe physical beauty (like a beautiful rose that will soon rot), is of little importance as the inner qualities speak more about a person. What good is one's physical beauty, when one is rotten inside?

He is forgiving of his enemies as he believes that

habitual hatred, even of those who have grossly wronged him, weakens the body. Hatred if continuously harboured in one's heart, consequently **kills** the heart. He is open, hospitable, and trusting—too trusting sometimes. He, for example, over trusted the white man.

He approaches matters from the standpoint of the heart dictating to the brain the course of action.

The African feels extreme discomfort to eat while his neighbour does not. Food and drink consumed and not shared cannot be enjoyed, so the African believes.

African Family—The Clan

Family is considered indispensable in African society. It is the essence of existence and the back-bone of society, without which Africans believe, there would be no society. It's considered the ultimate bridge between man and his god. Through it, he is permanently linked with the Almighty. One is considered a non-person in African society, unless one can lay claim to strong ties with a family.

In Africa, the family is more than man, woman, and the offspring—what sociologists in the West call the nuclear family. The father, mother, uncles, aunties, brothers, sisters, cousins, and all the relatives belonging to a singular family tree make up a family in Africa—or more appropriately a clan.

Such is the bond between close relatives in Africa that, for example, one refers to his father's brothers as *father* and his mother's sisters as *mother*. So it either one's younger father/mother or older father/mother. This is also to show traditional respect for one's blood relatives within the clan.

All these clan members can reside in each other's homesteads for as long as they wish—no questions asked!

Thus, all the dwellers of a group of houses neighbouring each other will be related one way or the other. No one lives far away from one's relatives in typical Africa.

Of course, the case is different for women as a result of marriage. But the men—the clansmen (as all male family members are regarded), are required by tradition to set up home near to the next of kin.

This is done in order to ensure full protection and help for every clan member. A clansman who goes to live in another village will often be looked down upon—and heaven forbid if he ever needed help! It'll be hard in coming from the relatives he left behind.

So every African lives, dies, and is buried in the same compound or village where he was born, according to custom.

Each clan has a customary head, who is charged with the unenviable task of law and order and the general well-being of every clan member. He settles disputes, presides over family gatherings, solemnizes marriages, and oversees funeral rites for the departed ones. Belonging to a clan comes with heavy responsibility in Africa. Often one's actions, omissions, and general behaviour reflect upon not just the immediate extended family but the clan as a whole. If a person is of good character and behaviour, then clan he comes from is held in high regard by the other clans.

INITIATION — BECOMING A MAN/WOMAN IN AFRICA

In most African societies, one has to go through the ritual of initiation at a certain age, in order to achieve manhood or womanhood. Until then, one is still considered a child however old he or she may be. One is also considered unclean, and may not fully partake in the daily activities of life within the clan. May not for instance, serve food or drink to the initiated, may not give advice on any matter or may not even get married because he or she is still *a child in the head.*

Where initiation rituals take place, the ceremonies are taken very seriously and often, this is a great occasion for the entire community to get involved.

Methods of initiation vary from society to society, and country to country. In some societies, only men go through initiation and vice versa.

Of those traditional customs still surviving to this day in Africa, initiation of youngsters in order that they may become men or women remains the most intact. Great importance is attached to these ceremonies, especially by the initiatees as they can't **wait** to be men and women in the eyes of society.

The equivalent in the West to initiation in Africa is being able to obtain a driver's permit or vote.

A young Masai about to face a lion in order to become a man

The Lion

*   *   *

In Uganda's traditional grouping of Bagisu, circumcision for boys is the means by which one gets initiated. For the Masai of Kenya, and in some parts of the Sudan and Swaziland a young boy of about sixteen coffee seasons throws himself into the bush bare-handed and kills a lion in order to become a man. If the lion kills him first, then he has made a mess of things! God rest his soul in peace!

In the small groupings of the Kalenjin in Kenya and the Sebei in Uganda, Somalia, some parts of Nigeria, and Egypt, the women are circumcised. This involves clitoridectomy (cutting some parts of the female organ).

Both rituals are *painfully* painful! No pain-killing herbs are applied prior to the operation. The idea here being that if one can withstand such excruciating pain, then one will be able to face up to whatever adversity that may come along in life. The initiatee must bear the pain without even so much as a twitch, for failure to do so brings shame to the entire clan. For a boy, this could result in being sent to live with his mother's clan. His failure to be brave is usually blamed on the mother's side. That it was the cowardice of his maternal uncles that made him be afraid of the knife!

As an inducement to be brave, the initiatee is given a number of gifts ranging from money, chickens, goats, cattle, to land. These will naturally help the youngster when it comes to setting up his own home.

The operation on boys is done by traditionally trained surgeons. Women surgeons perform operations on young

The author's clan (Banawodya) during circumcision ceremony

Author's mother with two of her sons and a relative before circumcision

Author's brothers going through the ritual of "touching the wound," to show bravery

Traditional circumcision surgeons

The author's brother during the actual operation—his face is that of a very brave young man.

girls. In the former case, women may attend the ceremony but men may not do so in the latter case.

Blood (and lots of it) is shed during the operation. This is important as the individual's blood dropping on soil, is seen as an act of establishing a bond with the land and being reunited with his ancestors.

With initiation, comes respect and recognition by one's community. The responsibilities of adulthood are also immediately placed on one's shoulders. The individual may now fully participate in the affairs of the clan such as offering opinion on matters, counselling would-be initiatees and presiding over some ceremonies within the clan.

Adjusting from childhood to adulthood within a short space of time, is never easy for the newly initiated. Often more responsibilities than one can handle are heaped on one's tender shoulders. But fortunately in Africa's close family set-ups, there are plenty of relatives to help the youngsters adjust to their new life.

For the boys, it is time to vacate the father's house and set up their own quarters within the compound. For the girls, it is time to get ready to leave the compound and get married. Marriage is imminent. Hardly three moons will go by after initiation before one is united in matrimony.

The other great achievement after initiation is that, on death, the individual's name will be given to a newly born child within the clan. But the individual must have been of good conduct in life. This is the prerequisite before the honour may be given.

MARRIAGE IN AFRICA
AND WHAT IT MEANS

Soon after initiation, one must get married in Africa as we have seen above.

> It is considered abnormal, unnatural, and un-godly not to be married. The decision isn't left to the individual, as such, but to the entire society

It is considered abnormal because it is **abnormal** to live without the opposite sex; it is unnatural because man and woman need each other for their physical and emo-tional needs. Moreover it is considered un-godly because God made man and woman and commanded that they unite in marriage to reproduce humankind. On these grounds, Africans uncompromisingly mandate marriage. No **ifs** and **buts**. One gets married or risks the wrath of the community.

Marriage is also seen as a stabilizing factor in one's life and as a test of one's maturity in living up to responsibilities to society. The responsibility requires everyone to take a wife or husband and bear and raise children to replace the departed ones. Africans also regarded marriage as a way of expanding the clan. Both clans of the marrying couple are linked up by this sacred act, thus strengthening both clans. The two clans become one big family, each responsible for the welfare of the other.

Marriage is also a status symbol in African society. One's status in society becomes greater when one gets married.

*   *   *

Arranged marriages are still common in many parts of Africa. Usually in these situations, the uncles, aunts and other notable relatives of a youngster will get together for close consultations as to who will be the most suitable partner. The youngster's character, temperament and general conduct are taken into consideration in choosing a suitable partner. This involvement by the relatives is to ensure that the right candidate is picked for their child, and most importantly, to ensure that the marriage has the entire clan's blessings.

Among the Gikuyu of Kenya, the bride to-be plays a prominent part in the marriage ceremony. The family of the groom-to-be comes to the home of the girl. They carry with them several gourds of (njohi) beer. In order to determine if the girl is agreeable to the boy's marriage proposal, she is asked by her family whether they should drink the (njohi) brought by the family of the groom-to-be. If she gives her consent, then serious negotiations between the two families get underway for her to get married.

Inter-marriage between people of the same clan is taboo in most parts of Africa. However, in some parts of the Gambia, Senegal, Sudan, Somalia and Ethiopia second and third cousins can marry each other.

Each family takes exraordinary care to check into the background of the other youngster, insisting on a clean background and nothing less.

Today, the tradition of arranged marriages is a lot more relaxed. The youngsters involved may now have some say in the whole matter. For example, if they didn't particularly approve of the chosen partner, they may voice their opinion. There was a time in Africa when one had to make do with whatever the aunties came up with. Things have changed these days!

*   *   *

In all this, the ability to have children is of paramount importance. For instance, if a girl came from a family where there are many known cases of infertility amongst the women, she would have a harder time convincing the boy's family that she would do better!

It's important in Africa to have children. In fact as soon as a young couple gets married, both families begin anxiously counting the moons. If three or four moons go by and they don't see any *swelling* round the waist of the girl, they go up in arms! Tragically, in Africa, whenever a couple is unable to have children, this misfortune is blamed entirely on the woman. Happily, things are beginning to change and men are also being regarded as *prime suspects* in cases of infertility.

Children in a marriage are seen as the only occurrence that can truly strengthen and cement a marriage. A marriage without children, will soon fall to pieces, the Africans believe. Why else would a man and woman be together?

With marriage, comes the respect of the clan and beyond.

One achieves instant adulthood with this single act. One then, the Africans believe, has made peace with God and paid his due to society. He then has the blessings of society and those of God.

*   *   *

That is how Africans saw marriage and in many ways, still see it today. As God's command and man's responsibility to obey the command! In most African communities, it is a tradition for the brothers of a married man to refer to his wife directly as *their* wife— metaphorically speaking! They can even touch her affectionately in symbolic expression of their love for her. But they may not *touch, touch* her That is a taboo! However, upon her husband's death, any of the surviving brothers or close relative may inherit her as his wife with the blessings of the clan.

Marriage in Africa means that tomorrow is taken care of, that the dead will be replaced by those being born as a result of marriage that the aging will be looked after by the children they bore in marriage, and that society as a whole will never die. Not when there's marriage and reproduction.

DOWRY AND BRIDE PRICE IN AFRICA AND WHAT IT MEANS

Dowry and Bride Price are still part of the marriage ceremony in Africa.

A lot has been written about them and often the meaning of the ritual is taken out of context. Let us distinguish the two before we go any further.

Dowry is an act by which the bride and her family bring gifts to the family of the groom, before marriage takes place. These gifts can range from money, jewelry, and cattle, to physical property such as land. Dowry is practiced in most parts of West Africa and in many parts of India.

Bride Price, on the other hand, is the act by which the groom and his family give various gifts to the family of the bride.

Western writers have wrongly interpreted this as 'buying' a woman but within African traditional custom it isn't, and that's what matters!

The bride price is a way in which the family of the groom says to the family of the bride, "Thank you for having such a beautiful girl for our son to marry."

> It is an act which obliges the man to take his marriage seriously and **not** for granted

This act also says, "I love you, I respect you, I will honour and protect you, I respect your family, and I'll be married to you until oceans turn into small rivers and mountains crumble into molecules!"

In some communities, if the bride is a virgin, then the number of gifts automatically multiplies. How the boy's family finds out is not through him telling them. They're more sophisticated than that! This is how they find out:

Two elderly aunts of the groom (who have seen it all), spend the first night that the couple sleeps together, underneath the bed. They generally have an idea what goes on during the night. But just to make sure their assumption was right, they carefully examine the beddings in the morning. If drops of blood are found on the beddings, then that's a good indication that the bride was a virgin. They announce the good news accordingly. There is jubilation on part of both families, especially on part of the bride's family. They can go around boasting that they brought up their daughter so well that the first man to *climb* on her was her husband! No small achievement by any means.

The next night, it's the turn of the bride's aunts to spend the night underneath the bed. This time, for totally different reasons. They want to find out whether or not their daughter has married a *real* man. They want to witness his performance! If in their estimation the boy's performance falls below standard, they report the sad news accordingly. Often this may lead to the dissolving of the marriage. What good is a woman to a man who can't live up to his tasks? Because of this, the boy's grandparents will have spent weeks coaching him on how to *satisfy* a woman. The bride's grandparents will have done the same with her.

In the rare event of the marriage failing, most of the gifts are returned. But more often than not, such strong ties will have been established between the two clans that the gifts are simply never talked about after a breakup. This is because marriage in Africa is more than an affair between two people. It involves both clans at every stage of the union. The bond between the clans will go on forever, especially where children are involved. The children then are the cement between the two clans.

Both Dowry and Bride Price play a significant part in stabilizing hence giving longevity to a marriage. The young couple is always mindful of the great expense their families went through in order for their union to materialize into marriage. No silly arguments will drive them asunder! It will have to be something major.

POLYGAMY IN AFRICA

Polygamy, a custom of having more than one wife at the same time, has been in existence in Africa ever since the beginning of humankind. That's a long time!

The custom has endured to this day and there are few signs to indicate that it'll not continue.

Polygamy is easily one of the most misunderstood customs in Africa. I know of no where else, (apart from the Muslim world) where this custom is practiced, making it quite unique and unusual. But of course everyone had read about King Solomon and his 700 wives! So it has happened elsewhere. The difference being that elsewhere, it was the exception rather than the rule. In Africa it's the rule!

Polygamy first of all ensures that everyone gets married and stays married. If the husband dies, then it is custom in Uganda, Sudan, Kenya, Zaire, and Tanzania that one of the brothers of the deceased marries the widow, as we saw earlier. If the wife dies, then her sister or a close relative becomes the widower's wife.

*   *   *

There are hundreds of stories about the origin of polygamy in Africa. Some are as simple as this one:

One day a man asked his wife for some water to drink.

"Go and fetch it yourself, isn't it enough that I have to open my legs for you?" She reportedly responded.

"I don't know why I ever married a woman such as you," he answered in disgust.

"I challenge you to go out there and find another woman *like* me!" She replied. He did! He married her identical twin sister! The three of them and their children, so the story goes, lived happily ever after!

The most sophisticated version goes like this:

Once upon a time, the women ruled Africa. They were the queens and empresses. Their rule was absolute and they answered to no one. Power eventually got to their heads. They started mistreating the men, making them work from sunrise to sunset without food or water. Often they

A young girl about to get married: if she's a virgin, the gifts to her family will multiply

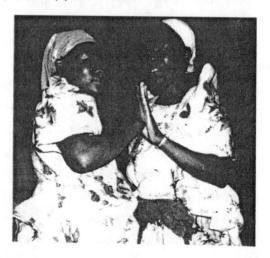

The first wife (on the right) is negotiating with the young girl to marry her husband, as his second wife

would have women attendants lashing behind them as they worked. One day the men revolted, but this only angered the women rulers even more. More severe punishments were dished out. The men got together and decided to do something about their plight. They met in the bushes for days and days but were still lost as to what to do.

Then one day, they heard a thundering voice from above them. It was God! He told them that he had heard their cries and was going to rescue them from the tyranny of the women. He commanded them to make every woman pregnant, starting with the attendants and then the rulers. The men did just that!

One night, while the women were asleep, the men made them pregnant, and while the women were pregnant, God handed power to the men. The men decided to take as many wives as they could and make them pregnant in order to contain them. The story concludes—that is how women lost power in Africa, and that is why men marry more than one wife!

*   *   *

How polygamy works in Africa is fairly simple. A man sees another woman he likes, talks to her, and tells her he intends to take her as his second wife, subject to his first wife's approval.

Tradition, from this point on, demands that he goes and informs his first wife about the 'new woman' in his life and requests that she starts the negotiations going. The first wife, with a few close advisers, go to check out the young girl. They interview her. They ask her questions such as: has any man ever *climbed* on you? Do you wash your bottom at least twice a day? Do you clean your teeth everyday? Do you know how to make a man happy in bed? Have you ever burnt food? Are you quarrelsome? They report back to the husband accordingly. All being well and the young girl passes the interview, the serious talking gets underway. The first wife is involved at every stage. She, by the way, must ultimately tell the clan that she approves of the girl for the marriage to take place without problems. When she finally gives her consent, traditional ceremonies take place and that is all there is to it. The man has a second wife!

He sets her up in her own house. The three of them get together to work out the days he should spend with each wife. Two days at a time, one week at a time—whatever. He must follow the timetable strictly. He must have his meals with the woman he is presently sleeping with. If he overstays with one woman, there is plenty of trouble—this is when things get upset!

If he decides to marry a third wife, the same process takes place. The two wives do the negotiating.

> All the children born out of these marriages belong to all the women according to custom. No distinction is made between the children. All the women are their mothers

Now and then the man will want to find out which

woman loves him most, or will miss him most should anything happen to him. Simple! He picks up a rope and runs towards a tree threatening to 'end it all.' The woman who struggles hardest to wrestle the rope out of his hands *loves* him most!

The women usually develop a close relationship. They become each other's adviser and confidant. They stick together through thick and thin.

The last time a man tried to beat up one of his wives, was the time he didn't soon forget. All the four wives ganged up on him and gave him a thrashing he talked about until his dying day!

The first wife will always be the most respected by every-one. Everyone including the succeeding wives refer to her as the *Big Mother*. Nothing gets done without her being consulted first by everyone. She is usually the central figure in the family, seeing to mundane things such as everyone's welfare, to bigger tasks like settling disputes within the home.

*   *   *

If a man wants peace in the home, he must first keep peace with the *Big Mother*! They wield the kind of power the equivalent of which is unknown in other societies.

Anecdotes about the origin of polygamy apart, polygamy has been accepted in Africa as a stabilizing instrument within the family. As we'll see later in the chapter when   we look at divorce in Africa, polygamy plays a big part in divorce being uncommon in Africa. It has effectively removed one of the most common grounds for divorce in the world—adultery. Adultery was no ground for divorce in Africa because there was no such thing as **adultery!** If a married man *slept* with another woman, often it would be the culmination of a relationship which was *aided* and *abetted* all the way by his wife!

> Polygamy in Africa, also recognizes man's weakness in his abilities to fight off temptation to have affection for other women. This is not to be interpreted as promiscuous behavior as promiscuity in African society is frowned upon

The Africans simply believed that if you didn't allow man to have more than one wife, you would have him running around **cheating** on his wife. Africans are of the firm belief that men, unlike their womenfolk, are naturally incapable of having one relationship at a time. Ask any African who gave them such ideas and the answer will be, "God!"

THE IN-LAWS IN AFRICA

In-Laws! There are strong customary laws which govern the relationship between in-laws in Africa.

The husband may not touch or be within a few feet of his wife's mother in some societies. The same goes for the wife in relation to her father-in-law. This is not so much out of dislike for the in-laws as it is respect for them. The opposite sexes of both sides may not look straight into each other's eyes. This is to avoid any possibility of the two developing physical attraction for one another.

They may not speak directly to each other—or if they must do so, it must be through a third party. If they accidentally come into physical contact with one another, then a white goat must be slaughtered at once to calm the spirits. If on the other hand, the touching is intentional, on part of the husband, then there are problems! How dare you touch your mother-in-law when you already sleep with her daughter! Isn't it bad enough that you *undress* the daughter?

A fine of up to ten chickens, two goats, one cow, and ten thousand cowries,* is summarily imposed and must be paid at once.

If the father of the husband *touches* his daughter-in-law, then there are even bigger problems. He is summoned to appear before the traditional court to answer the charges.

* *Small shells formaly used as money*

If he's found guilty and a first offender, he is fined a total of twenty goats, five cows and fifty thousand cowries and told in no uncertain terms to keep away from his daughter-in-law and find another woman. If the offense is repeated, he could be excommunicated from the clan altogether.

The brothers of the wife must be treated with utmost respect and awe. They have the power to recall their sister if they are dissatisfied with the treatment they get from the brother-in-law.

When they come visiting, a whole chicken with gizzard boiled or roasted must be placed before the eldest brother. He may devour the whole chicken or share it with his young brothers and the host. On leaving the home, they must be given several live chickens to take with them. Only then will they have been properly entertained.

ROLE OF MAN IN AFRICA

Man, Africans believed, was created by God to be His personal representative on earth. In him, God entrusted the care of all His creations on earth.

> God then bestowed upon him His gifts of intelligence, prowess, kindness, honesty, and courage. He commanded him to be the guardian of His kingdom on earth

But as to exactly how man initially physically came to be on earth, there are many beliefs in Africa, each with all kinds of explanations.

In East and Central Africa for example, the Africans believed that in the beginning man lived with God in heaven. God did everything for him. All that man had to do was obey God. Then one day, man disobeyed God. God then decided to send him on earth to fend for himself.

The belief continues that God then told man that he could have a second chance to go back to heaven and live with God again, if he was good on earth; if he didn't kill fellow man; if he didn't steal; if he didn't lie to or about fellow man and if he honoured God's name.

But before man left to come to earth, he asked God for a companion on earth. God gave him woman—to love, protect, and honour, especially to protect!

> In Africa, women walk behind men. This is because the man must be in front to ward off any danger that may come the family's way

Stories from other parts of Africa are not too dissimilar and all revolve around man as the dominant force. Man is portrayed in all these beliefs as being powerful, courageous and second only to God in human potential. Needless to say that African societies are unbashfully male oriented.

The giving of names to newborn babies is done exclusively by men in most African societies. Burial of the dead, consultation of the oracles, hunting for food, preparing the fields for plantation, building, herding cattle, slaughtering of animals and poultry, administering of certain traditional medicines to the sick and praying for rain are mainly male roles in Africa.

Role of a Woman in Africa

A lot of twaddle, out of ignorance I presume, has been written about the role of women in African society. Their roles have been at the best reduced to children bearers and little else, and at worst, to domestic workers! This is utter nonsense.

Here's the truth!

Ancient Africans believed that one of the reasons God made a woman after making man, was that He wanted to improve on His art.

> God wanted that art to reflect among other attributes; physical beauty, intelligence, tenderness, compassion, patience and tolerance

That God had tried but miserably failed to get this combination in man. All he had got were muscles, a bit of a brain and very little else. Forget about beauty!

Africans also believed that God knew that man would be lost without a woman. That he would be incomplete hence would only behalf human.

In modern times, the woman in Africa remains a powerful figure. She is the essence of being and existence. A man is not considered a **man** in Africa unless he has a woman beside him. A home without a woman is looked down upon and often the object of ridicule by society. The home is also shunned by people because it is considered unblessed hence cursed. Who in his right mind would want to visit a home not graced by the presence of a woman, Africans would ask.

All women in Africa are regarded as *mothers*. Not in the limited sense of bearing children, but in the larger sense of being the ones God blessed with the gifts of continuity of the life line and the linking of man with fellow man. A woman, who even though may have not borne children of her own, is often referred to as *mother* in most African societies. A man who beats up on his wife is considered by society to be weak in mind and utterly lacking in moral character. How dare you beat up on God's finest creation? Society wants to know!

So that crap you have read about the woman in Africa being a second class citizen, is no more than just that—*crap*!

Of course, men in Africa have the upper hand when it comes to issues which affect the larger society. But the influence and power of women in so far as stability in the homes and the survival of society are concerned, cannot be minimized.

Traditionally, the kitchen area is exclusively for women and men are forbidden there. A man who is known to go to the kitchen is often despised by both women and men in most parts of Africa. What kind of man goes to the kitchen to pick quarrels with women?

Once in Africa, men believed that if you wanted anything done **quickly**, you asked another man. But if you wanted anything done **properly**, you asked a woman!

The woman is the central figure in the home

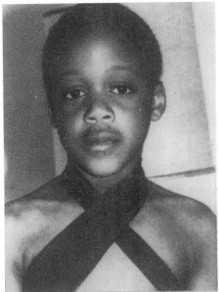

Children are a big exultation in African society

Women are regarded as the peace makers in most African societies. When men quarrel and can't agree on an issue, usually it is women who intervene to bring the two sides to an accommodation. In times of sorrow, everyone including men and children look to the women for comfort. When an African swears, he swears in the name of his god and his mother in that order. The woman is yesterday today and tomorrow!

*   *   *

This poem Camara Laye wrote about his mother while a student in France, best typifies the esteem in which the woman (mother), is held in Africa:-

"Black woman, woman of Africa, my mother, I am thinking of you...

O Daman. O my mother, you who bore me upon your back, you who gave me suck, you who watched over my first faltering steps, you who were the first to open my eyes to the wonder of the earth, I am thinking of you...

Woman of the fields, woman of the rivers, woman of the great river banks, O you my mother, I am thinking of you...

O you, Daman, O my mother, you who dried my tears, you who filled my heart with laughter, you who patiently bore with all my moods, how I should love to be beside you once again, to be little child beside you!

Woman of great simplicity, woman of great resignation, O my mother I am thinking of you...

O Daman, Daman, you of the great family of blacksmiths and goldsmiths, my thoughts are always turning towards you, and your own thoughts accompany me at every step.

O, Daman, my mother, how I should love to be surrounded by your loving warmth again, to be a little child beside you...

Black woman, woman of Africa, O my mother, let me thank you; thank you for all that you have done for me, your son, who, though so far away, is still so close to you!
The African Child, 1954 by Camara Laye..
I can't do better than this poem.

ROLE OF CHILDREN IN AFRICAN SOCIETY

Children are a big exultation in African society. Their coming is always eagerly awaited by society and by individual communities in particular. To say nothing about the pride a family feels with this blessing.

All doubts about a marriage soon disappear with the arrival of a child. To the Africans, the marriage is then properly consummated. The relationship between the clans of both the husband and wife, is cemented forever, the moment the child is born. For the blood of both families is intermingled through the child. Never again will the two clans ever see the other as anything less than family. Not when they are related through the blood that runs through the veins of the offspring. From now on until eternity, they are united by the ties of consanguinity. Children in Africa don't stay children for very long. They are encouraged to assume adult roles in society as a way of testing their character. There is a saying in Africa that, *"A bull that will grow to be fertile and healthy, can be detected at birth."* So the way a child behaves in childhood, Africans believe, will have a bearing on his behaviour in adulthood. At most celebrations, it's the children (usually boys of about nine or ten coffee seasons old) who do the drumming and playing of various musical instruments.

Most of the minor tasks within the home are performed by children. Fetching water from the river, herding cattle, carrying messages from one clan to another, and generally attending to the needs of adults. Respect for adults can't be over-emphasized.

> Children are not expected to talk back to adults in African society. It's a cardinal sin for a child to engage in arguments or cross words with his elders. The reason being that the adults saw the sun first so they know better!

Perhaps like in no other society, children in Africa are also seen as an insurance policy for the parents. When they get old and are unable to look after themselves, tradition demands that the children take care of them.

BIRTH & NAMING OF A CHILD IN AFRICA

In most parts of Africa, the day a woman finds out she's pregnant is considered the day that God spoke to the family in person. It's the day when God says to the family, *"I have heard your prayers for a child and this day I grant you your wish!"*

Africans are notorious for praying for things. So naturally, prior to a woman conceiving, rains and rains of prayers will have been said.

In some societies, when a woman finds out that she has a 'stomach,' it is custom that her family knows first. Her mother and aunts are informed first. This is because it reflects well on the family and gives great joy and pride to the rest of the clan. In Africa, it's important for a clan to have a reputation of being **fertile**. The news then spreads like fire on dry grass among the relatives of both clans.

Both clans prepare hundreds of family male and female names for the expected child. Everyone is happy! The mountains are happy. The rivers and lakes will rejoice and swell beyond their banks. The trees will throw longer shadows. The grass will be greener. The animals, the insects, and the birds in the sky will sing louder than ever. The rains will come down thundering like the sound of gunfire. The sun, the stars, and the moon in the sky will declare peace with one another—Africans believe these three are vowed enemies!

That with a child on the way, nature has triumphed over

the evil spirits that hinder man's procreation and growth. So the news of a baby on the way isn't taken lightly in Africa.

Various rituals will be performed as a way of saying, "Thank you," to the spirits—meaning God. A cow could be slaughtered and portions of meat placed under a sacred tree. Healers prepare special herbs for both the expectant mother and the baby to insure that they are healthy throughout the pregnancy.

The expectant mother may not do certain things for fear of 'upsetting things.' She may not, lose her temper or quarrel with anybody. She may not speak evil of anyone. She may not, in some societies, engage in sexual intercourse, especially in the advanced stages of the pregnancy. She may not fetch water from the river because the child may be born with nothing but *water in the head!*

In some societies, the woman goes to live with he relatives until she gives birth. Specially trained midwives perform the honors of delivering babies. Men are never allowed to witness childbirth. This is one area where men feel is none of their business so they stay clear. The only men who are allowed to stay nearby are the healers to perform certain rituals in difficult deliveries. But in most cases, they will have already taken precautions to insure that everything runs smoothly.

Prior to the woman going into labor, the healers from the woman's clan will take a chick from its mother and keep it covered up for several days without food or water. Poor thing! If the chick survives the ordeal, then the chances are the child will survive not only babyhood, but will also grow up to endure adversity.

This ritual is practised in Senegal, the Gambia, Cameroon, Zaire, and Uganda.

If it's a baby boy, then the whole village is engulfed in sounds of special drums to greet the arrival of a 'clansman' as all baby boys are regarded. This is because baby boys are seen as the ones who, unlike baby girls, will grow up to keep the clan's name, join the ranks of other men of the clan to preserve that which has been passed down.

When it comes to naming a child, great care is taken to insure that the child is given the right name according to custom. A name that must reflect what the experts decide is the true character of the infant. These experts spend days with the child studying its characteristics to determine who of the hundreds of departed relatives the child resembles most physically. They determine whether the child will be quiet, outspoken, gregarious, moody; caring, daring, cowardly, adventurous, a leader, you name it! On the basis of the conclusions, appropriate names are chosen for the child. The men then take over at this stage.

The naming of a child is done in the evening, about the same time as the chickens come home! The oldest among the *name givers*, takes the infant in his arms, whispers appropriate words in the child's ears, lifts it above his head and loudly announces all the names. The child's first name is that of a departed relative it resembles most.

Apart from the names that reflect the child's physical looks

The beating of the drum is mainly done by children

Sacred place of worship

and character, tens of other names from both sides of the parents are given to the child. So it's not unusual in Africa for one to have easily up to twenty names. In Africa, one may not necessarily inherit his father's last name like in other cultures. A child may also be given a name or names that best describe a happening at the time of birth. For example a male child born during unusually heavy rains in some parts of Uganda and Kenya, is called: *Wafula*—meaning rain.

AFRICANS AND THEIR CONCEPT OF GOD

One of the most monstrous lies perpetuated about Africans by Europeans is that they didn't know God!

> That until the missionaries arrived, the African lived the life of a pagan and the existence of God was unknown to him. This is a huge mountain of a lie!

The Africans knew God. They wouldn't have had names for God if they didn't know Him in the first place. Here are examples of the names for God in different parts of Africa:

Country	Common Names For God
Burundi	*Imana, Mukama*
Gambia	*Yalla, Alah*
Kenya	*Mungu, Ngai, Nyasaye, Wele, Mulungu*
Liberia	*Yalla, Yensuah, Glapor, Alah*
Mali	*Irkok, Amah, Alah*

Nigeria ....*Alah, Chukwu, Olisa, Chineke, Oluwam, Obasi*

Rwanda ....*Imana, Mukama, Omukama*

Senegal ....*Rook, Yalla, Alah*

Somalia ....*Rabbi, Alah*

Tanzania ....*Mungu, Mulungu, Ruwa, Ishwaga*

Togo ....*Mawu*

Uganda .... *Wele, Katonda, Mungu, Ruhanga, Rugaba, Ori, Nyakanasaye, Mukama, Umuwangafu, Nakyizolongo, Wemungagyi.*

To the Africans, God is ubiquitous. He is the beginning and the end. He has power over everything. He gives and takes away. He creates and destroys.

Africans firmly believed that in the beginning, God created the universe, then man, woman, trees, mountains, rivers, lakes, animals, rain, and sunshine in that order. Each creation complimenting the other. That because He created all these things—they all represent Him on earth.

> So in Africa, God is rain, trees, mountains, lakes and all nature

God is also believed to be merciful as well as capable of administering punishment. He is believed to be pure, infallible, holy, a genius and super-wise.

When things go wrong, Africans believe that God is angry with man. Such natural disasters as earthquakes, death, thunderstorms, excessive heat, or heavy rains that destroy crops and animals are signs that God is angry with man. In these cases, offerings of all kinds are made in order to calm God's anger.

Thus all occurrences, good or bad, are attributed to God. Everything happens because God so wishes them to happen or else they wouldn't happen. The birth of a child, is God's wish. The death of someone, is sometimes regarded as God's wish for better or worse.

It was considered ungodly to do anything without first asking God's guidance. Africans therefore are notoriously prayful. This is considered the only way one gets closer to God—through prayer.

The following were common beliefs about God in Africa before the missionaries came:

God The Creator

That He created everything on earth, as well as in heaven and the sky. That nothing dead or alive ever came in this world without going through the hands of God.

God the King of Kings

That all kings, queens, and chiefs were directly under God. The kings, in particular, were believed to be direct descendants from God. That He anointed them to be His personal representatives on earth administering justice for His creation.

God The Merciful

That He is merciful and kind. That in spite of man's wicked ways, God still shows him mercy in dispensing justice.

God the Father and the Mother

That God ultimately was everyone's father and mother at the same time. In some parts of Africa, God is actually directly referred to as Father both spiritually and biologically.

God The Super-Human

That He is super-human and therefore never dies, never makes a mistake, never takes a bribe, never gets tired, never lies and always patient with man—in spite of himself

God The Judge of All Humankind

That ultimately, He will be the true impartial judge of all humankind. That whatever judgment man passes over fellow man, will be reviewed by God again.

God the Never Ending

That He will always be there—He was there yesterday, is there today and will be there tomorrow. Never sleeps a wink, always there!

All nature represent God on earth because He created them

The heir apparent being installed following the death of his father

God the Healer

That He heals all humankind's wounds—spiritually and physically. He heals sorrow and sadness. He heals suffering and pain.

God is Love

That He loves abundantly. That He loves even those who don't love Him. That through love, all is possible.

SEX IN AFRICAN SOCIETY

Sex was considered sacred in African society. For a man and a woman to engage in it was seen as a commitment to each other.

Casual sex was despised and frowned upon. Africans believed that sexual intercourse is the ultimate in male and female relationships. It seals and solemnizes it at the same time. Thus, if a man has sex with a woman, according to African custom, she becomes his wife by this single act.

She may, at this point, move in and live physically with the man following traditional ceremonies, or choose to live with her family. But forever, she will be considered the wife of the man she *slept* with.

If children result from this 'loose relationship,' then this upgrades the relationship from that of lovers to parents. The children then have parents and are treated by society no differently.

There is no translation in African languages for the word 'illegitimate.' A child born of a man and a woman is God's child like any other. The nonsense of 'out of wedlock, therefore illegitimate' doesn't apply in African society, thank heavens!

Sex education in most African societies is left entirely to the grandparents. They teach the grandchildren the basics and are always on hand for advice. This stems from a long traditionally held custom which defines the relationship between a grandfather and his grandsons as his *brothers* and his granddaughters as his *wives*—metaphorically speaking. Using the nouns 'brother' and 'wife' enables the grandparents and grandchildren to engage in sex talk without any inhibitions or embarrassment.

HOMOSEXUALITY AND RAPE

Homosexuality is taboo in African society. Ten years of exhaustive research across the continent didn't produce any evidence of homosexuality having been part of the African way of life.

Indeed, hardly any translation of the word 'homosexual,' exists in most African languages. Equally, there is no direct translation in African languages for the word 'rape' as *to force a woman to have sex,* was regarded by Africans as an abominable act, a revulsion, utterly immoral, degrading, and most ungodly!

> Africans have a name for almost everything they do that is part of their culture. The absence of direct translation of the words could only suggest that homosexuality and rape were never part of African culture

Who in his right mind would want to climb on another man when he could have as many wives as he so wished. Who?

Men in Africa, for example, hold hands, but only as a *brotherly* gesture. Yet Western 'scholars' have misinterpreted this as an act of homosexuality. Yet another cruel lie!

However, I am not so sure today, with strong influence of Western **culture** in Africa! Things regrettably have changed a lot these days. The white man has imported a lot of bad manners and habits into Africa. For instance, there was a time in Africa when it was unthinkable to beat one's wife. Today, especially in urban areas, men beat their wives in the kitchen!

DIVORCE IN AFRICAN SOCIETY

Divorce was never allowed or encouraged in ancient African society, save in the most extreme cases. Everything possible was done to save a failing marriage. This stemmed from a long held belief that the act of marriage, was God's wish. To destroy it therefore, was the most ungodly thing to do. Indeed there is no direct translation for the word *divorce,* in African languages as it was never part of African custom. You can only describe the occurrence as the couple *no longer live together*. There is no direct translation for 'divorce.' Also, marriage in Africa is more than just an affair bet-ween two people. It involves both clans of the marrying couple. In a sense, the two clans get married to each other, if only metaphorically speaking.

Before the marriage, moons and moons would have been spent to make sure the marriage *should* take place. The backgrounds of the couple would have been meticulously checked. Oceans and oceans of prayers would have been said. Rituals on top of rituals would have been performed to make sure nothing ever goes wrong with the marriage.

One of the common rituals performed in most parts of Africa, involves chickens.

A hen from the family of the bride and a cock from the family of the groom are obtained. The "couple" is then put to live together as *man and wife* under close scrutiny by the experts on these matters. They observe every move the chickens make. They observe the way they get along or otherwise. The chicken couple must demonstrate propensity to have children or else this can lead to the marriage being called off.

Usually about three moons are taken to observe the chickens. If the union is seen as successful, then there is nothing to stop the impending marriage from being successful. The couple's compatibility or the lack of it is gauged by the behaviour of the chickens which respectively represent them in this experiment.

Another way that divorce is discouraged in Africa is the way marriages are conducted. Marriage is an affair of great interest to both families of the couple. They take pride and pleasure in it. If a problem develops between the couple, both families are called in at once to arrest the problem while it is still young. So a couple's problem becomes both clans' problem. Tradition encourages open discussions of any problems that may crop up.

If a man is notorious for beating his wife, he is told to stop at once or the next time he lays a finger on her, the wife's brothers and uncles will beat the hell out of him! If the wife is disrespectful to her in-laws, then she is advised to clean up her act or risk being bewitched by the sorcerers so that she may never have children!

The only extreme circumstances under which divorce might be granted are if the wife elopes with another man, the couple's incompatibility or if the marriage endangers the welfare of the children and threatens to sever the relationship between the two clans. Only and only then will divorce be allowed.

Here, the chiefs take over. They summon a meeting of both families. They exhaustively listen to the evidence and grievances. They talk to the couple in private. On the basis of their findings, the marriage is annulled. The children by custom remain within the father's clan. This is the only way that they can inherit any property. The mother, however, may visit them whenever she wishes.

After divorce, the two clans continue to live as relatives

and further inter-marriage between them is encouraged—especially to replace the one that has just collapsed.

DEATH AND FUNERAL RITES IN AFRICAN SOCIETY

Africans believe that in the beginning, God intended man to live forever and that death only came as a consequence of something that man did.

There are several myths in Africa surrounding the origin of death. In some parts of Africa, the belief is that the gift of eternal life was forfeited by man when he ate the forbidden fruit. In others, the belief is that man simply disobeyed God and went his own way, and as a punishment God sent him death. The most amusing of these beliefs is that man was supposed to live forever until he beat his wife! God said to him: "Death to you!"

But Africans also believe that God being merciful, said to man (as we saw earlier in this chapter), if he repented his wicked ways, he could live again forever. Only this time he would have to live close to God in heaven. Whatever myths surround the origin of death, it is painful for the loved ones the world over. Africans, how-ever, deal with it in their own way which is uniquely African.

*   *   *

Whenever the death of someone occurs in Africa, the cause of it is addressed immediately. Witchcraft and other evil magic are suspected in most cases. If death was caused by accident such as falling off a tree, then that tree is suspected to have been smeared with lethal herbs. The tree is cut down immediately. If the death is by drowning, then special witchcraft is suspected to have been performed to swell the river so that the victim would drown while swimming or drawing water. No one from the family of the victim ever swims or draws water from that river again. If it's death by illness, then either slow poisoning of the victim or slow killing witchcraft are suspected to be the cause of death.

The body of the victim is laid either inside the house or outside on the verandah for public view. Those suspected of being behind the witchcraft that killed the relative are not allowed anywhere near the body. If seen, they are chased away at once.

Women do the wailing whereas the men sing songs, often in praise of the departed relative.

In Africa, a man must never shed tears in front of women or children. To do so, would be to appear weak before the very people he is supposed to protect!

The body is displayed until all the relatives have gathered and paid their respects. Custom requires that they give gifts of money to the bereaved family to help defray funeral expenses. A relative who fails to show up for the funeral is often accused of having bewitched the deceased! The relative may be reprimanded the first time this happens. However, if he becomes notorious for not attending subsequent funerals of departed relatives, he may be chased away from the clan altogether. Often, such a relative will end up living among his mother's clansmen.

Throughout the mourning period, which in all may last up to three moons, the close relatives of the deceased may not do any work. Such tasks as fetching water from the river, gathering fire wood and cooking, are eagerly performed by the distant relatives.

The following day after the initial shock of a death, the atmosphere of sadness is soon replaced by laughter. This is one way Africans deal with tragedy. Through laughter! The relatives will recount anecdotes about the things the departed relative did or said. This goes on until the day of the burial. Then the sad atmosphere takes over again. For their relative is about to physically depart forever from them. More wailing by the women and more singing by the men.

When the deceased is a person of note, as a chief or king, the burial often assumes a carnival atmosphere. The burial is accompanied by music from drums and dancing by all those assembled for the funeral. Often the dancing will go on until the early hours of the morning. Only then will the important person have been *properly* escorted to the next world!

The body then is prepared for burial. It is washed, shaved, nails cut off, anointed with special oils, wrapped in clothes, and placed in the grave by the male relatives. Often in the backyard of the house.

It is tradition in many parts of Africa to bury the dead with their most treasured belongings. Africans believe that the dead live in the next world and need provisions to take with them. Long ago, kings and chiefs were buried with their servants and wives for companionship. The burial of a man with a family, is immediately followed by the ceremony of succession. The heir apparent who will have been groomed for the role, is installed. The ritual involves the successor swearing allegiance to the clan and often out of respect for the deceased, assuming all his names. This is one way that ensures that one never really *dies* in African society.

Next come the funeral rites. Within the family, a child of the same sex as the departed relative will have been born.

Somehow in Africa, babies born immediately after a death strike a remarkable resemblance to the departed relative. Maybe the healers fix it!

Women shave off their hair. The men shave off their beards. The hair growing again is an indication that the relative had a good heart and will continue to live in the next world. There are cases where the hair never grows back. This is interpreted as the relative having been of bad character and therefore died a *real* death!

Close relatives will stay with the bereaved family for moons on end. Finally to break the period of mourning, a big feast is organized. Cows, goats, sheep and chickens meet their death in the process!

VISITORS AND STRANGERS IN AFRICAN SOCIETY

In African society, a visitor is anyone who arrives at one's door. All he does, is arrive! He may not be previously known to the hosts, nor his visit previously announced!

It is custom then to make the visitor welcome and entertained immediately—**no questions asked!** Why the person may have come, how long he intends to stay, and where he intends to go after the visit is over is none of the host's business. The business of the host is to entertain the visitor.

> In Africa, it is considered immoral to turn away or deny hospitality to anyone who comes to your door. Tradition demands that the person is looked after first of all, and if any explaining is needed, that is left entirely to the visitor

After being made welcomed, the visitor is then given water to drink because he must be thirsty. In the good old days, locally brewed beer would be given to the visitor to wet his throat for starters.

It is customary for the host to take a sip of the drink before handing it to the visitor. This is to ensure that the host hasn't *tampered* with the drink in any way! The visitor then proceeds to perform the libation by pouring a few drops on the soil as an act of sharing with the ancestors.

A chicken would be slaughtered for the main course.

During the conversation, the visitor would then, out of courtesy, reveal who he is and where he comes from.

Today, tea is the commonest way a visitor is initially entertained. It is considered highly offensive in Africa to ask anyone if he *wants to eat* or *drink*. Africans believe that to be a stupid question! Does one need to be asked if one needs to eat?

A mugful of tea plus two sugars and milk, a bunch of bananas, yams, cassava, and nuts are gracefully heaped in front of the visitor. Successive mugfuls of tea keep pouring the visitor's way until he turns the mug upside down. That is a sign that he has had enough.

Traditionally in Africa, women serve food to men. In most parts of Uganda, Tanzania, and Malawi women kneel while doing so. This also happens when a woman is talking to or exchanging greetings with a man or older woman.

In some societies, if it is a male visitor, such as a chief, and he is not related to the hosts, part of the entertainment is being given a young girl to *entertain* him. How can a big man sleep alone? Won't he feel cold? It is also part of the African culture, for a visitor to sire a child in the village he is visiting. For that will be proof that he did actually *visit* that village and sought to establish kinship between his village and that of his hosts.

Failure to sire a child in the hosting village, will cast serious doubts as to the visitor's traditional diplomacy and virility.

Because of this important part of our tradition, it is possible for one to have relatives as far away as thirty villages.

When the visitor expresses the desire to leave, tradition demands that he's encouraged to stay longer. Often a casual visit may result into a man marrying a girl from the host family. This naturally leads to the union of his clan and that of his hosts. The visitor, from just turning up at the door unites two clans. Who in his right mind can find fault with that? Everyone is happy!

As we saw earlier in the chapter, this is how Europeans were welcomed into African society. The trouble was that they *urinated* on that hospitality!

AFRICAN MEDICINE

Unfortunately, African medicine was wrongly referred to by Europeans as witchcraft. This in spite of the fact that for centuries, Africans had used it and it had effectively cured illnesses. As we saw earlier in the chapter, Cecil Rhodes was cured by African traditional medicine—when European ones had failed.

Traditional African society has thrived on African medicine. This medicine is in form of liquids, herbs, bones, leaves, roots, plants, trees, certain birds, and animals. The medicine is either administered in straight form or blended with various components to achieve the desired results.

There is medicine for every known illness—physical as well as spiritual. Some medicines may be applied directly to the patient, others through mystical powers. This depends on the type of illness.

Mental illnesses, misfortunes, and barrenness are exclusively treated through mystical powers. Personal injuries to the body are treated directly with application of herbs.

African medicine is also used in such a way that it can stop certain bad things from happening. Just as Africans are notorious for praying, they are equally notorious for their reliance on traditional medicines as a guide and weapon. Often homesteads are 'treated' with preventative medicines to ward off thieves and evil spirits.

There are also medicines which a person may wear directly to the body for good luck. There are medicines that can

Traditional African medicine

The drum (ngoma) is at the heart of African life

cure infertility in women or can cause it. There are medicines to create wealth and prosperity. Medicines to cause harm to one's enemies. Medicines that can enable one to foretell what is going to happen in the future and medicines that are used in travels and numerous other aspects of everyday life. In almost all rituals performed in Africa, there's an element of medicine involved. Rainmakers, for instance, use bones and ash from medicine trees to bring rain or stop it. Fortune tellers use medicine chickens of a peculiar feathering in their work..

Happily and fortunately to this day, in spite of the intrusion of Western medicines, African medicines still remain at the heart of African life.

AFRICAN HEALERS

As everyone knows by now, African healers are infamously known as witch doctors.

The Oxford Dictionary defines the word "witch" as "a woman said to use magic, especially for evil purposes."

Now, listen to me carefully, my dear reader. Here are some points to consider: the word, "witch" is hardly an African word, so one deduces that it appropriately applies to the culture whose language the word comes from. Secondly, African healers are both men and women, but the word is defined as applicable exclusively to women. The conclusion being that the wrong word was applied to the wrong people in the *wrong* place at the *wrong* time!

The dictionary, by the way, "educates" us further by defining "witchdoctor" as a "medicineman," especially among primitive peoples."

My contention here is that at no time were my people primitive. Not after they had given birth to civilization as we know it today, as we saw earlier in the chapter.

> Therefore the labeling of African healers as witchdoctors, was at best misleading in content and, at worst, malicious in motive

As we have observed above, these healers can either be men or women. Their training takes an average of ten to fifteen rain seasons.

As is common with most healers, the craft will have been passed down from parents who also practiced medicine.

Every village has a healer within everyone's reach. Their reputation depends on the successes or failures in treatment of illnesses and misfortunes. There are good as well as bad healers. A lot depends on the scope of their knowledge and general expertise.

Most healers operate within their homes. Others have set up independent offices from where they practice medicine.

Consultation is strictly private. Their fees mainly depend on the nature of illness or misfortune. Their fees tend to be high when they have to go to the patient's home. Payment for services rendered, could be in form of chickens, goats, cows, or even land. They carry their tools with them when they go out and are often accompanied by young trainees.

Healers are usually highly regarded in society because of their expertise and wisdom. They are therefore looked up to as leaders in their own right.

They also perform religious rituals, act as marriage counsellors, give advice on how to avoid trouble, and generally give clues as to why things go wrong; e.g., crops failing, recurrent illness, infertility, deaths of people and animals and so on . . .

MUSIC AND DANCE IN AFRICAN SOCIETY

Africans are notorious for singing and dancing. Most joyful, as well as sorrowful occasions, are accompanied by music and dance.

The drum (ngoma) is the central musical instrument, and beating it is quite an art learned over many years. Often the craft is passed down from father to son and generation to generation.

Traditional Africa relies on the drum and its music in every walk of life. Sending messages, calling people to gather, announcing a death or birth of a child, burying important people; initiation; naming of a child; working in the fields and wrestling competitions, are instances where the drum is used.

Drum music would accompany men going to war and the music would be played in the background during combat urging the warriors to fight on to victory.

Furthermore, singing and dancing in Africa are a form of spiritual demonstration. The dancing is seen as a celebration of life over death. Often God is worshipped through music and dance. That through dance, the entire body and soul are involved in prayer and thanksgiving!

Most joyful as well as sorrowful occasions are accompanied by
music and dance. God is also worshipped through dance

4

Captivity & Colonialism:
European Glory, African Tragedy

THE EARLY EUROPEANS IN AFRICA
—First Phase of Exploitation

A t the outset, I want to make one thing absolutely clear. The Europeans who first ventured into Africa, far from being explorers and missionaries, were mere common criminals and bandits who went to Africa with the sole aim of robbing and looting the continent on behalf of their governments in Europe. As the subsequent events show, there was no mistake as to the actual intentions of these men and their governments. Africa was seen as a new *kill* and no efforts were spared nor chances taken to ensure that the prey stayed firmly in the claws of these blood thirsty men.

So the likes of Vasco da Gama, Speke, Stanley, Samuel Baker, David Livingstone, and Captain Lugard to mention a few, set out to **teach, Christianize** and **civilize** the African. Between them, these so called explorers and missionaries, a lot was done to pave the way for the eventual exploitation of Africa.

They came heavily disguised as traders, missionaries, and doctors. Under the guise of these honourable professions, enough damage was inflicted upon the continent as to cripple it for many, many years to come!

> In the name of Christianity and civilization, enough hideous acts were committed as to make those of Judiath Escariot and Adolph Hitler put together laughable! Heavy stuff you may think, but it's the brutal truth!

The lures of wealth and domination easily permitted Europeans to treat Africans as animals not even worthy of the most basic respect and consideration.

The full story of human trade will never be known but what is known, makes macabre reading. The lynchings, raping of women, and the general savagery that accompanied the human trade were horrifying enough. But the near permanent distortion of the African's image was to have far more devastating consequences later. His mind was conditioned to despise everything about himself. His colour became the crime he committed in the eyes of the Europeans his new *masters*.

The Europeans arrogated to themselves the role of *civilizers* of the African. Set upon in a self-righteous fashion to redeem him from his 'wicked' and 'primitive' ways. This 'righteous-than-thou' attitude has persisted to this day. The relationship between Europeans and Africans, therefore started off on the *righteous* against the *wicked* note with the Europeans being the righteous, and the Africans being the wicked! The African couldn't have started off on a worse note!

When one examines the situation that obtained in Europe, it is possible to comprehend why Europe turned to Africa as the source of supply of human resources for her economic development and imperial expansion. What is hard to fathom, however, is the extent to which Europeans went to destroy Africa and her inhabitants.

The plan, therefore, was simple—human trade was meant to rob Africa of her most able-bodied and mental resources. Missionary work carefully prepared the African mentally for subjugation. Colonialism put the final nail in the scheme of suppression and exploitation! There can be no denying that the exploitation of Africa started with the first ship which carried Africans into captivity to plantations in America and the West Indies during the sixteenth century. In effect Africa has been exploited by Europe since this period!

Nearly five hundred years of exploitation, exploitation, and more exploitation!

HOSPITALITY AFRICAN STYLE

Europeans were welcomed by the Africans who went to great troubles to make them feel at home, as we have seen in the previous chapter. It is part of African culture to treat strangers as visitors. This informal part of our culture enables the stranger to enjoy unlimited degree of hospitality and entertainment regardless of whether or not he was initially invited.

So it was that kings and emperors happily, or unwittingly, welcomed the early European **visitors** to their courts and palaces and lavishly entertained them. No questions were asked, nor was any hostility showed to these men who "walked on water by ship."

It is said that King Afonso of the Kongo, after the first Portuguese had entered his kingdom, made them welcome. He wrote several letters to the King of Portugal, reassuring him of the safety and the help he and his subjects would accord to his emissaries. King Afonso also sent for missionaries to come to his kingdom. King Mutesa I of Buganda did the same. All this, in good faith!

Perhaps the African's abstemious habits and his open-handed welcome and acceptance of the white man, was to be his first undoing! It certainly made him an easy target. Maybe he should have been less trusting and more questioning as to the white man's intentions in Africa.

His hospitality was abused by the Europeans and mistaken for *inferiority*. The Europeans believed that the reason

Colonialism in Africa: Europeans divided up the continent and then helped themselves to it!

the Africans went to great lengths to play host to them, was because they (the Africans) felt **inferior** to them, the Europeans. How mistaken they were!

HUMAN TRADE

Human trade has to rank as the greatest tragedy to befall a race and a people. Human trade has been witnessed in other parts of the world, apart from Africa, but where it differs is the scale and the brutality that accompanied it in Africa. For over two hundred years, ships shuttled between Africa on one hand, and Europe, America, and the West Indies on the other, carrying human cargo in conditions even Alex Haley was lost for words to describe. It has been estimated that for every ship-load of captives, barely half survived the trip. Some died from starvation, some from beatings, and others were merely hustled off the ships if they were found to be too ill to be of any eventual economic advantage to the owners. The sharks in the seas were to be treated to African flesh for a long time to come!

Prior to departure for unknown lands, European bishops would denigrate religion by *blessing* the shackled African captives and the ships before sail. So that no matter what happened to them, their souls had been sanctified.

> And these were supposed to be men of God!

The logical questions to ask in the saga of human trade in Africa are how it all started, and why it happened?

Naturally for human trade to have flourished on the scale it regrettably did on the continent, certain factors had to be responsible. Human trade largely succeeded by conquest and trickery on the part of the invading Europeans.

It was wrongly assumed that Europeans simply popped up in Africa and found a helpless and indolent people to whose rescue they had come. And that the African in his helpless state, was better off being taken as a captive than left to perish in his miserable surroundings. Utter nonsense!

With their superior weapons, Europeans found the task of conquering Africa easy. The task was made even easier by the feuds that existed between various kingdoms and states in Africa. The spears, bows and arrows were no match for the guns in the African's attempt to resist European invasion. It is true that in some parts of Africa, during the epoch of human trade, some African rulers cooperated in the sale of their people as captives.

> But it has to be emphasized that this was because of the tricks used by Europeans in their bid to conquer Africa

If only these African rulers who participated in human trade had known half the experience captives were to undergo, it is doubtful that they would have been such willing participants.

＊   ＊   ＊

One of the tricks Europeans used in human trade was to employ traitors who escalated conflicts between Africans of different states, and then war would ensue. The need for more sophisticated weapons would a rise and then the warring parties would inevitably turn to the Europeans for supply. The Europeans would demand Africans to work in Europe and America in exchange for the guns. Then Africans would unwittingly exchange fellow Africans for guns!

This nicely thought out trick worked until Africans had weakened themselves through constant warring, leaving Europeans to simply help themselves to the continent with no one to defend it. Then through local agents, Europeans would carry out human trade with themselves in supervision.

This is to the extent which Africans participated in human trade. The white man having firstcreated the conditions and the necessity for it—the necessity being the economic expansion Europe was undergoing at the time, as we saw earlier. The boom in the European economy created a need for labor—*cheap* labour. Europe saw it fit to turn to Africa for the supply of that cheap labor. This then started the trail of ships carrying African captives (not slaves) to work on plantations in the Americas and the West Indies.

This is how every African man and woman came to be in Europe, the Americas and the West Indies. First captured, then shackled, then shipped, and then enslaved by these 'God fearing' and 'civilized' men who **discovered** Africa!

CAPTIVES NOT SLAVES

Africans captured by Europeans have wrongly been referred to as 'slaves.' They were **captives**—repeat **captives**, not slaves. The mere fact that they were captured and taken to foreign lands against their will, did not then, or now, render them slaves. It is my contention that to refer to these hapless captives as *slaves* is to erroneously infer that they were actually slaves at the time of their capture.

There were no slaves in Africa before the European invasion. Therefore only, and I mean only, captives could have been taken out of Africa!

Similarly, to refer to them as slaves having reached their destinations on the plantations under individual white 'ownership,' is to imply that they *accepted* the status of captivity. True, they were **treated** as slaves. They were slaves, in other words, only in the **minds** of their white captors. No more, no less! This continual reference to Africans in the West Indies and Americas as descendants of slaves, has been perpetuated with grave psychological consequences for African peoples all over the world. At worst, it's a distortion of facts. At best, it only serves to reinforce the so-called superior race attitude on the part of whites on one hand, and the inferior race feeling by Africans on the other.

Undoubtedly, the success of captivity depended upon captives being forced to accept the degrading status of 'slaves.'

> As long as they saw themselves as slaves, they would think, act, behave, and function **as slaves** amid great rejoicing on the part of their white captors

There would be no desire on the part of the African to question his grossly underprivileged position, nor the will to better conditions for himself.

The brainwashing of the minds of the captives was therefore essential in the whole exercise. The very first thing that happened to every African captured and sold was being made to assume the name of his/her so-called *master*. There was fierce resistance to this, and as Alex Haley has told us, Kunta Kinte resisted being called Toby in place of his revered African name. Kinte's determination to hold on to his African past, however, was only temporary. In order to use him as an example, he had his foot amputated as a warning to the others. Would you believe this was done by *civilized* people?

This degree of savagery by whites was soon to succeed

in breaking the spirit of the die-hards and resistors among the captives (remember, **not** slaves). Kinte is said to have been offered the alternatives of either being castrated or have one foot amputated. He bravely elected to have his foot amputated rather than lose his manhood!

It is very hard to estimate accurately to what extent African peoples were handicapped by captivity and colonialism.

> But perhaps it's not an exaggeration to say that the lack of economic development on part of Africans wherever they may be, is directly attributable to the success of captivity and colonialism—and now neo-colonialism. Believe it or not!

As we have clearly seen in the previous chapter, Africans were not lazy and intellectually lacking as they were made out to be. We were capable and economically well developed and independent. Our level of civilization compared favorably with that of any other continent at the time. Perhaps in certain respects, more civilized! For a people who were once capable of the kind of development now being reluctantly acknowledged by some Western historians, captivity and colonialism must have had far more devastating consequences than has hitherto been acknowledged.

Captivity and colonialism, without any shred of doubt, succeeded in rendering African peoples helpless and dependent. They reduced the African to a near half being, who perpetually had to depend for his survival on the goodwill of the white man. His abilities to invent and create, and to think and act independently, along with his dignity were spitefully annihilated by the white man during captivity and colonialism.

> Every where one goes, African peoples are still in chains. Whether back home in Africa or anywhere else, their rights and freedoms, be it economic or social, are not guaranteed

This state of affairs is no accident. It was deliberately created to suit the white world at the expense of the black world. The degree of development in Europe and North America today is the extent to which Africa was, and still is, exploited by these two continents.

> They were, after all, the main beneficiaries of captivity

They are so advanced and wealthy because Africa was, and is, so under-developed and impoverished by them. Captivity and colonialism carefully saw to this state of affairs.

*   *   *

Nobody was more aware of this than Marcus Garvey. His understanding of captivity and colonialism and their effects was to be the basis for his arguments later in his struggle to redeem the African world. It was as a result of captivity and colonialism, Garvey rightly argued, that the African found himself in his lamentable position, politically, socially, and economically.

No sooner had the last ship carrying captives docked at New York Harbor than the missionaries were taking up positions in Africa!

MISSIONARY WORK IN AFRICA
—SECOND PHASE OF EXPLOITATION

Colonialism might not have succeeded to the extent that it did in Africa without missionary work.

If there ever was a time when the African and his culture were parted, (almost for good) was during the epoch of missionary work in Africa. It was during the same period that Europe established her firm grip on Africa, and that the white man established his so-called 'supremacy' over the black man. It was during the same period that the African had his mind impregnated with ideas which rendered him helpless and split his personality right down the middle—ideas which were designed to convince him of the 'wickedness' of his cultural ways

Ideas which were intended to make him aspire to the whiteman's culture and traditions which were presented by the missionaries as being superior to his own!

Among many things, what also spurred on missionaries to come to Africa was the grand idea of converting the 'pagan' African to Christianity. To make him turn away from his 'primitive' ways and seek salvation through Christianity.

Two hundred years of captivity had greatly weakened Africa. Captivity had left behind a demoralized people, so missionaries seemed at the time to have arrived at the most opportune moment. Their overt association with the 'anti-slavery' campaigns made them enormously popular with the Africans. They were seen as the 'good guys' and men of God against the bad guys who indulged in captivity. These men who wore heavy boots, khaki trousers with safari tops, and mushroom-like hats (to protect them from the sun) had virtually the whole continent at their mercy to do with it what they liked.

They came heavily armed with Bibles, and through these, they would colonize the mind of the African for a long time to come. After captivity it was important for Europe to control the mind of the African. With the mind of the African firmly in his hands, the white man would be *armed* with the most lethal weapon with which he would exploit him for a long time to come. Nobody has power over another person unless that person can control the mind of their victim!

No where else did the missionaries score the same degree of success as they did in Africa. Their success in Africa was near total. In India, the Indians, to a greater extent, were able to hold onto their culture. But Indians did not experience captivity. The Japanese, on the other hand, fiercely resisted Christianity.

Captivity had reduced the whole continent of Africa to a toothless giant by the time the missionaries came. A vacuum had been created and any nice sounding ideas would do!

EUROPEAN NAMES

The first task the missionaries performed in the "civilization" process was to baptize Africans after conversion. As a mark of being a Christian, the African was told he had to have a Christian name, such as Richard, David, Robert, Wilson, Keith to mention but a few. What the African didn't realize, however, was that these names were nothing more than English, French, or Italian names. They were no more Christian names than Nangoli or Mandela!

> Sadly, such was the success of the mental colonization of the African that to this day, he goes round calling himself by these offensive European names

However well meaning and God fearing an African may be, if he/she does not bear the name Charles or Elizabeth, he or she is considered a pagan! This is more or less taken for granted on the continent.

Having successfully turned him into a Christian, the missionaries proceeded to preach to the African the ways of Christianity. *Love thy neighbor; thou shall not hate;*

the love for money is the root of all evil. Unbeknown to the African at that time, the European neither loved his neighbour nor was himself immune from avarice! When the African finally found out the truth, it was almost too late—the damage had already been done!

> As well meaning as the missionaries might have been, they all agreed on and were convinced of one thing—that the black man was inferior to the white man in every way

Samuel Baker, a spy disguised as a missionary, seems to have summed it up for all of them when he said;

"The natives of tropical countries do not progress, enervated by intense heat, they incline rather to repose and amusement than to labor. Free from the rigors of winters, and the excitement of changes in the seasons, the native character assumes the monotony of their country's temperature. They have no natural difficulties to contend with—no struggle with adverse storms and icy winds and frost-bound soil, but an everlasting summer, and fertile ground producing with little tillage, excite no enterprise, and the human mind, unexercised by difficulties, sinks into languor and decay."

Men such as these completely ignorant of Africa's glorious past, happily contented themselves with such beliefs. They then saw it as the white man's burden to *civilize* the African.

The tragedy of it all is not so much that the white man believed the black man to be inferior to him, but that the black man was actually *persuaded* of this unfortunate belief. This belief set him on the course of dependence on the white man to this day.

It was this total dependence by the black man on the white man which made Garvey tick! Ridiculed though Garvey may have been, nearly five hundred years since the first white man set foot on African soil. His words ring true today as they did when he first uttered them in the nineteen-twenties.

There can be very little doubt that the greatest success of missionary work in Africa was to make the African depend for his survival and development on the white man. Because the missionaries were firmly entrenched in Africa, colonialism was a matter of when.

COLONIALISM
—THIRD PHASE OF EXPLOITATION

The colonization of Africa by Europe in the second half of the nineteenth century was simply the final icing on the cake.

This third phase of exploitation was, perhaps on close examination, the most devastating for Africa. The master plan by which the continent would be exploited by Europe was laid during this era. As a result, the African today best articulates himself in non-African languages, and wallows in Western fashions of dress. With the oven-heat of Africa, he boils himself in woolen suits and strangulates himself with the white man's rope that he calls 'tie' in the name of smartness. He has no faith in his own abilities; he depends on other races' achievements in science and technology. He rains praises on other races' advancements but never stops to think of doing the same; he has cultivated a culture of dependence on other races for survival rather than carve out a niche for himself.

> Worst, he has placed his destiny firmly in the hands of those who hold him in contempt in the first place. He is in the danger of losing his only soul!

After the infamous 'scramble for Africa,' the continent was soon divided up between Britain, France, Portugal, and Germany as the principal robbers.

Later, after the First European War, last century, Britain and France emerged as the main thieves in Africa. Germany had lost the war and her stolen colonies as well. They were divided up between Britain and France. The map of Africa was soon re-shaped into so-called British Africa, French Africa, and Portuguese Africa in that order. Britain was the greediest as she stole more land than anybody else. Each *mother* country set up methods and systems by which the stolen territories would be exploited.

> Whatever the cosmetic differences in the methods of administration, the Europeans had one objective in common; they were all in Africa for what they could get out of her—pure and simple!

Thus, the fact that the French had the policy of **assimilation** and the British the policy of **indirect** rule was neither here nor there. At the end of the day, the hapless African, whether in so-called French Africa or British Africa, had been equally and thoroughly exploited.

*   *   *

In a heated debate on colonies in the French National Assembly in 1885, one Jules Ferry, then Prime Minister, put it simply this way: *"The nations of Europe desire colonies for the following three purposes:*

1. *To have access to the raw materials of colonie;*
2. *To have markets for sale of the manufactured goods from home country and*
3. *To have a field for the investment of surplus capital."*

Ferry may have been speaking for the whole of Europe.

*   *   *

This third phase of exploitation by Europe was also to characterize the relationship between the two continents, which has carried on to this day.

Given this kind of economic order, Africa, tragically, has been kept permanently underdeveloped and crippled. Europe, with her superior technology, has sustained this economic imbalance which favours her. To redress this imbalance, Africa will need to restructure all systems left behind by the colonial powers. These systems which still exist today in Africa, were not meant to benefit the African, but the settlers and their home countries. More later in chapter nine.

What you have on the continent now are economies which have a natural built-in dependence on industrial economies of Europe and North America.

There is hardly what could be called freedom or independence in Africa—not until full economic independence is attained.

The greatest exponent of the African's full political, economic and industrial independence was one Jamaican, son of Africa, called Marcus Moziah Garvey. Let's now look at him—and find out who he is . . .

Part Two

MARCUS MOZIAH GARVEY
(1887-1940)

5

Marcus Moziah Garvey
Birth and Early Years in Jamaica

B y the red brick house they owned, Garvey played with his little white friend from next door, the home of a Scottish settler. The two kids chased each other about the compound totally oblivious to each other's color, and were united by their common ignorance about racial prejudices. Never before had it occurred to them throughout the time they played together that because one was white and the other black, was sufficient reason not to play games.

Suddenly, the little girl's father emerged from the house enraged. Like a hungry vulture, he pounced on the little girl dragging her by the ear while screaming to the house.

"Let go, let go, daddy!" She cried out.

"How many times have I told you not to play with that

nigger? How many times have I told you that you might catch diseases from him?" He was raving mad!

"But daddy, his name is not *nigger*—his name is *Garvey*, my friend!" She pleaded with her father.

"I don't care what his name is, he's still a *nigger*, understand?"

"Daddy, what is a *nigger?*"

"I don't know, but he is a nigger. Uncouth, uncivilized and dirty. You are white, pure, and clean!"

"Daddy, I'm not clean: my hands are filthy, look ..."

"Shut up!"

Garvey, meanwhile, looked on frightened, and then ran to his mother crying uncontrollably.

"Mom, that Mr. McClister said my friend Imelda should not play with me because I'm a nigger and have diseases!" Sobbed a young Garvey.

"No—Moziah. You're no nigger, and you have no diseases. You're black and beautiful just like your friend is white and beautiful. Look at that painting on the wall." Garvey Sr. liked collecting paintings and had them hanging all over the house.

"You see, that painting has different colors. That's why it is so beautiful."

Young Garvey had stopped sobbing by now.

"You see, Moziah, God intended to beautify the world by having different races of people, just like the painter intended to beautify his picture."

"Mom, can I go and show Mr. McCliser our painting?"

"No Moziah, he will not understand that either. Just be proud of yourself and your color. You come from a line of great people. Your ancestors were men of the Golden Stool. They mothered world civilization. They invented the art of writing, building with stone, drawing and painting, when white men still slept in caves..."

For young Garvey, that one incident was to trigger off a one-man crusade to change the world and bestow upon it a more human face! The ugly side of humanity had just manifested itself before his very young eyes. Something had to be done!

A Child is Born

Maybe it was a blessing in disguise that this particular incident took place. Maybe it was pre-planned by some mighty forces too hard to comprehend by man. Whatever the case, Garvey ceased thence on from being an innocent little black boy next door. He assumed about him the kind of character which, if only Napoleon Bonaparte had had, Waterloo would have been for keeps—at least for the time being.

Marcus Moziah Garvey was born in August 17th, 1887, in the small town of St. Ann's Bay, Jamaica. His parents, Marcus and Sarah Garvey, had eleven children altogether, Garvey being the youngest. However, tragedy struck the Garveys and all their children, except Marcus Garvey Jr.and his sister Indiana, died in childhood.

Garvey Sr., was a man of obstinate disposition and displayed a rare kind of fortitude in face of danger or opposition. He was demonstratively non-conformist and the only time he appeared in church was on funeral occasions. Long sermons in church appealing to the emotions rather than to the intellect of man, bored him to tears. He preferred the practical side of life and every-thing else he could immediately relate to.

He was a direct descendant from the Maroons (originating from the word *Cimaron*... meaning the 'wild ones' or more appropriately the unyielding ones, as we will soon see). Quite conceivably, this had a lot to do with his unyielding character. The Maroons, as they are popu-larly known in Jamaica, were African captives who bravely refused to submit to the degradation of slavery. They escaped into the hills of Jamaica as soon as they were off loaded from the ships and set up homes there as free men. They, on a number of occasions, fought off British military assaults consequently forcing the British to relent. They won their right to live as free men preferring instead to be ruled by their revered chiefs as they had been back in Africa.

Both Garvey Sr. and his wife Sarah, were of unmixed African stock. This was later to prove a set-back for Garvey Jr., in his campaign to rally all African peoples of the world as we will see later.

Although not highly educated, Garvey Sr. was nonethe-less, endowed with a keen intellect—a gift he passed on to young Garvey. He read extensively, and it is said he was happiest when locked away in his room with his books. He also acted as a local lawyer and was held in very high esteem by the dwellers of St. Ann's Bay.

Sarah Garvey, on the other hand, was the direct oppo-site of her husband. She was kindly and submissive by nature. Unlike her husband, she attended the local Wesleyn Methodist Church regularly, and according to Garvey Jr., "Was always willing to return a smile for a blow, and ever ready to bestow charity upon her enemy." A neighbor who knew the Garveys well, described Sarah Garvey as one of the most beautiful women she had ever seen. Her skin was black and soft as velvet; her eyes were jet black, large, liquid and sad; her voice was gentle and caressing; and her figure well shaped and erect. Her beauty was the talk of the town!

The Garvey family was reputed to be very wealthy in the early years of Garvey's childhood. It was not long, however, (like most Africans who had made it), that the Garveys' wealth was destroyed by jealousy of the whites. Garvey Sr.'s own obstinacy and pride, had partly contributed to the withering of the family fortune.

Mr. Gaul, a newspaper publisher, had for twenty-years supplied Garvey Sr. with a daily paper as a *free* gift, at least that is what Garvey Sr. understood it to be. However, when Mr. Gaul died, and in winding up his estate, the executors decided Garvey had to pay for the papers he had been receiving for twenty odd years, and proceeded to send him a bill for $150. A colossal amount at that time.

Characteristically, he declined to pay the bill inviting the executors to sue him if they so wished! They did just that. Garvey lost the case (however mitigating the circumstances), and after still refusing to pay, he had one of his properties attached and sold for far less than market value.

This irritated him beyond measure. He grew less and less patient with everybody, acting quite irrationally at times. Constant fights with neighbors over seemingly trivial matters led him into costly litigation, often losing the cases and consequently losing all his lands but for the house where he lived with his family. Of all this, Garvey Jr. was to write later, "He once had a fortune, he died poor!"

With his confidence badly shaken by the loss of his wealth, Garvey Sr. subsequently took less interest in his family, preferring instead to lock himself in his private study, reading and meditating. This, in effect, meant that Sarah, his wife, had to take charge and young Garvey and his sister Indiana were largely brought up by their mother. She had to do all kinds of odd jobs to supplement the family income. She made delicious pastries from coconuts and guavas and sold them in the local market. Young Garvey often accompanied his mother to the market. The two consequently developed a very close relationship.

*   *   *

Of this different mixture of parents, Marcus Moziah Garvey was born. The story has it that when he was born his mother prophesied that he would grow up to lead his people like Moses. When it came to naming him, she had naturally chosen the name Moses, after the Moses in the Bible. Garvey Sr. however, had other ideas. Not one given to ecclesiastical tendencies, he disagreed. Being a believer in astronomy, he preferred calling him Marcus, like himself.

He argued that "Any boy born under the planet Leo the Lion, is bound to be a leader in his line." Rather than fall out over it, a compromise was struck between the parents. The boy was given the middle name of Moziah because it was less biblical. Garvey Sr. called him by no other name but Marcus. Sarah, however, insisted on calling him Moziah because it was nearer in sound to Moses.

For what the prophesy by both parents was worth, it couldn't have been very wide of the line. Perhaps Garvey might be forgiven for believing that his was a life destined for a special mission to his people: the African people. "I was born and ushered into a world of sin, the flesh and the devil," he once wrote. Characteristically, he saw it as his solemn duty to do something to better the world.

When he came of school age, he was taken to St. Ann's Bay Primary School, which was a walking distance from home. Trouble was around the corner.

Here, he encountered race discrimination against Africans by whites, and was greatly disturbed by it. Immediately on arrival to the school, he confronted the headmaster, a white settler from England, and urged him to do something about discrimination in the school.

"You must understand, Sir," he once lectured to the headmaster in his office, "that the fact that you happen to be white doesn't give you any right to behave like God, any more than the fact that I happen to be black should mean I should submit to your whims. We are here to be judged by our mental intelligence or the lack of it, but not by our skin color."

Infuriated by this direct challenge from a 'nigger,' the headmaster showed him the door and warned him to behave himself or else! Not one to be intimidated, Garvey responded by writing big posters, posting them on all school walls with the inscription:

> "Message to the White Folks...Stop racial discrimination, we are all God's children...you have no more claim to this world any more than we Black Folks have..."

For this, he was summoned to the headmaster's office for a dressing down. He told the headmaster in no uncertain terms that he would continue fighting race discrimination until it was completely eradicated from the face of the earth. He slammed the door behind him and left!

Racial distinction in the school meant white pupils and black pupils sat separately, and ate different type of food (black pupils' food of interior quality). Black pupils were not allowed to swim in the school pool; but were told to go and swim in the sea.

One day, while swimming at sea, one of Garvey's friends drowned and was never seen again. Distressed when he learned of the tragedy, he went to school the following day and organized a strike by black pupils.

Garvey was again summoned to the headmaster's office, only this time, not for a dressing down, but for a *chat*. The headmaster promised to see to it that he was not discriminated against, i.e., he could swim in the school pool, sit with white pupils and eat the same food as they. Garvey was in no mood to compromise. "It' s either for *all* or I'm not interested in your special privileges—my people would never forgive me." He went ahead with the strike and called on all black boys and girls to sit wherever they pleased, swim in the pool and stop doing menial work, (which only they did) and generally refuse to cooperate until racial distinction was ended.

The school came to a standstill. The headmaster responded by giving in to all Garvey's demands. Only then did normal classes resume! He had won the battle but not the war.

Garvey became an instant star among his fellow pupils, and even won the admiration of white ones. He was never whipped by any, but made them all respect the strength of his arms and physique. He was stockily built and manly in looks even at that young age.

Education for him came from all sources. He never relied upon what he was being taught at school alone. He studied privately and often he would lock himself up in his father's study. He went to two public schools in St. Ann's Bay and eventually to two high school colleges. His teachers found him not the easiest to teach as he was well ahead of his times.

One day he embarrassed a geography teacher by asking him a question about Africa he couldn't answer. That same teacher one day privately reminded Garvey that he was at school to *learn* but not to *teach*!

*　　　*　　　*

The family's acute financial position was to deny Garvey a normal childhood. While still at school, he became a printer's apprentice. So he worked and went to school at the same time. But it was not to be long before he was forced to leave school altogether.

Mr. Burrows, his godfather, took him on to learn printing in his firm on full-time basis. Mr. Burrows also owned a large well-stocked library on the same premises, and Garvey eager to learn, made full use of it. On alternate days during lunch time, he would go sit by the sea and meditate. By this time, he had enough experience in life and intelligence to manage men. "I was strong manly," he re-called later, "and I made them respect me. I developed a strong, forceful character and have maintained it still."

Prospects for career advancement in St. Ann's Bay were pretty slim. As much as he loved his job and working for his godfather, he felt, nonetheless that a move to Kingston would offer wider scope. At the age of eighteen, he moved to Kingston to seek work.

Wake up Black Man

For a supremely self-confident and articulate lad of 18, it was not long before he found work. He was soon employed as a printer with one of the leading firms at the time, P. A. Benjamin Company. Here, he made quite an impression on his employers and was promoted rapidly. Within two years and at only 20, he became the master printer and foreman—a position most people achieve at a much older age!

Garvey had not been a foreman long when the printers union called for a strike for wage increases and better working conditions. Having realized his remarkable leadership qualities, and the impact his involvement in the strike would have, the management secretly offered to increase his pay. This was with the view to dissuade him from joining the strike, but unfortunately for the management, Garvey was not one to compromise over principle. He turned down the offer and threw in his lot with the strikers. With the considerable weight that Garvey threw into the strike, the workers won handsome wage increases and better working conditions.

For his role in the strike, he was *white-listed** by the company. From then on, Garvey was almost unemployable. Although he left P.A. Benjamin Co. to work for the government, this was not to be for long. The vocation for leadership was more than he could resist.

During this time, it was becoming increasingly difficult for Garvey to settle down in a job properly. His ever-curious and questioning mind, was leading him more and more further afield, albeit unconsciously. Kingston had naturally opened his eyes to the realities of race discrimination against Africans.

For the first time in his life, he was witnessing, on a mass scale, the injustices meted out to his people with such degree of arrogance, that he could hardly stomach it. "I can't remain a spectator with my arms folded behind me in face of such blatant arrogance," he said to himself.

For Garvey, there was only one thing for it; to become actively involved politically and to travel as much as finances would allow, and get first hand accounts of situations obtaining in other parts where fellow Africans lived. With what finances he could lay his hands on, he braced himself for a tour of the other islands in the West Indies. The African must wake up!

* *White-listed as apposed to blacklisted, because the listing was by a White man and not Black.*

YOU MAY BE THE GREATEST, BUT I'M THE LATEST

Before he left Jamaica, he started a magazine called appropriately: *Garvey's Watchman,* and helped establish a political organization called National Club, which also published a fortnightly periodical known as *Our Own.* These principally, were aimed at the African readership. So he embarked on a one man fact-finding mission.

The first country he visited outside Jamaica was Costa Rica. Here, he found the conditions of African workers on British-owned plantations so appallingly inhuman, that he decided rather characteristically, that something would have to be done pretty fast.

First, he arranged a secret meeting with the workers on the plantations to get first-hand accounts of life on the plantations. He heard such accounts as long work hours (from sunrise to sunset) without breaks, women being raped by white men, beatings, and starvation. He had heard enough! Immediately he went to the capital, Port Lemon, to meet with the British representative there.

He found him cold, unsympathetic, and unwilling to discuss such 'trivial' matters. Garvey was incensed by this negative and cavalier attitude by the consul. As he walked out of the building from his meeting with the British Consul, he was thinking aloud, "No white man would ever regard the life of an African as equal to that of a white man."

Garvey, inevitably, was convinced beyond a doubt that being African automatically meant subservience to the white man. He was not ready to give in on that one!

He faced one dilemma at this point: how was he going to rally African public opinion and then see what could be done about their common plight? A solution was around the corner. While still in Costa Rica, he started a paper called *La Nationale* to get his message through. This did a lot to awaken most Africans and to start questioning their humiliation by those who had taken it upon themselves to be **masters** in somebody else's house!

From here, he went to Ecuador, Nicaragua, Spanish Honduras, Colombia, and Venezuela. Everywhere he went, it was the same old familiar story of the African being oppressed and exploited! He had seen enough. Garvey hurried back to Jamaica to see about enlisting the government's support to alleviate the suffering of his people.

As might have been expected, the British officials in Kingston were unimpressed and in no mood to entertain 'one over-enthusiastic nigger purporting to represent the Africans.' Everywhere he went, he was greeted with, "You are black," as if he needed reminding!

Completely disillusioned with everything in the West Indies, Garvey packed up his belongings and set sail for England in 1912, on another fact-finding mission to learn about the conditions of Africans in other parts of Europe's so-called colonies.

Marcus Garvey... his devotion to the African cause knew no bounds

AFRICA   FOR   AFRICANS

First, Garvey went to London, England. He set upon working immediately having settled himself in some reasonable quarters in the West End. He met with and talked to African seamen, scholars, and Africans from all walks of life from all over the world.

Soon after he arrived, he met an Egyptian journalist called Duse Mohammed Ali, publisher of the *Africa Times* and *Orient Review.* The two men became instant friends. Ali was particularly impressed by Garvey's concern for the plight of fellow Africans not just in the West Indies but all over the world. He invited Garvey to work on his magazine as an editor. By this time he had developed a keen interest in writing and the power of communication. The two talked through days and nights about the plight of the African throughout the world, and what, if anything, should be done to change things.

Through his many conversations with Duse Mohammed (a very learned man) and his magazine, Garvey learned more about the conditions in the colonies in Africa. About the same time, he came across *Up From Slavery* the autobiography of Brooker T. Washington—the sage of Tuskegee Institute in Alabama. This book by Washington, among other things, fired him with the greatest enthusiasm and inspiration to do something actively to help free fellow Africans wherever they may be.

Through it, he had a first hand account of the conditions of Africans in America. They were equally appalling. Despite the end of captivity, very little had changed.

Whites still happily treated Africans as subhuman beings, "who should be grateful that they were alive in America and being civilized, and not starving in the jungles of Africa!"

Garvey was rapidly becoming global in outlook. He found it difficult to disassociate one situation from another as far as African peoples' experiences were concerned.

He conceived the idea of self-help and self-reliance at this time, believing that the only way Africans were going to truly free themselves was through achievement. He was becoming restless so he decided to take time off from the magazine and travel around Europe. He found the same old story!

He hurried back to London and invited Ali to his apartment one weekend. "Muhammed, my brother, we have to do something if our race is to survive!" He went on, "If Europe is for Europeans, Asia for Asians, then "Why not Africa for Africans?" Ali looked on despair— as if to say that's the way it is ... This in effect started the **Africa for Africans** philosophy.

Of all the philosophies espoused by Garvey, none was as misunderstood as **Africa for Africans**. To whites in particular, it smacked of something racist about it. Whereas it was in order for them to say that Europe was exclusively for Europeans, it was *wrong* for an African to say the same about Africa. What our white friends failed to appreciate was that if Europe was for Europeans and Africa for Europeans as well, there would be nothing left for the African! Or did it not matter that the African went without. Talk of double standards!

His doom of being a race leader dawned upon him in London after he had travelled through almost half of Europe. One day while walking alone in a park (except for the onlookers), he burst out in a deafening voice ... "Where is the African man's government? Where is his king and kingdom? Where is his president and country, and his ambassador, his army, his navy and men of big affairs?" He could not find them so he declared ... "I will help to make them!"

For what he could do, his young and ambitious mind led him into flights of great imagination. He now desperately wanted to see African men and women no longer treated as serfs, dogs, and slaves, but as men and women of affairs making an impression upon civilization and causing a new light of dawn upon the human race.

He could not remain in London a day longer. Enough was enough! What he had just seen in Europe was the last straw. His brain was now afire. There was a world of thought to conquer, and he had to start before it became too late and the work had to be done. In June of 1914, the year of the outbreak of last century's First European War, Garvey now inspired, angry, restless, determined and supremely confident, boarded a ship at Southampton bound for Kingston, Jamaica.

THE DREAM MUST COME TRUE

Garvey was board the ship now. Inside himself, he felt inspired and yet angry, supremely confident and yet hopeless, determined and yet in despair.

"I must do something ... I must do something, God willing." He told himself over and over again. His doom of being a race leader had just dawned on him in London. The ship was too slow. He couldn't wait to get home. Restless, he paced up and down the deck to kill time. Talking to whoever cared to listen to his aspirations for the African world.

Soon, he met a West Indian family returning from Southern Africa. Garvey, quickly made friends with the family. "Tell me brother, tell me, are conditions as bad as I hear for our brothers and sisters there?" He asked his new friend in a desperate voice.

"Indescribable, indescribable brother. The white man treats the African worse than shit!"

Of what his West Indian friend told him on the ship Garvey later wrote; "He related to me such horrible and pitiable tales that my heart bled within me ... I must rescue mother Africa, I must rescue the African from the white man." With that, he bade his new friends good-night and retired to his cabin!

He threw himself on the bed, lying on his back and looking up to the ceiling. He tried to sleep. Sleep wouldn't come. He opened his window. With his head in both arms and resting his elbows on the window, he looked at the sea. The sea was calm. He could hear himself thinking. He threw himself on the bed again, lying in the same position. Suddenly, ideas started flashing through his head.

One after the other, they poured in his head. He looked at the octagonal clock on the wall by the window, the minute hand touched twelve and with both hands in that position, the clock struck midnight! Like a huge storm that had engulfed the whole room and him, an idea revealed itself to him ... the idea of the U.A.I.A* (The Universal African Improvement Association). "That's it, that's it, that is what I will call it!" He cried out! Such a name, Garvey thought would embrace the purpose of all African humanity. Thus, to the world, a name was born, a movement created, and a man would become known!

For Garvey, the creation of this organization and all its activities, would occupy him practically for the rest of his life. He never was to have a moment's rest from now on. The hour had suddenly come for him to put into practice all his thoughts and dreams for the African world.

Within a week of arrival back in Jamaica, he founded the U.A.I.A., with a program of uniting all African peoples of the world into one great body to establish a country and a government absolutely their own in Africa, the land of their birth. The dream must come true!

Now, unashamedly a public figure, Garvey set on a course which would soon create him friends as well as enemies, and admirers as well as critics.

To Garvey, however, there was an urgent job and it had to be done regardless of the consequences or risks involved. Whether or not it meant taking on the whole might of the white world, and pay a price for it, so be it. He was on the march and unstoppable!

---

* *U.A.I.A. Although popularly known as U.N.I.A., the word NEGRO is anathema to Africans, besides Garvey himself really meant African.*

6

Marcus Garvey

The Man and The U.A.I.A.

G reat leaders come and go. They influence the times in which they live and those long after they are gone. They are a rare kind of breed, moved by events often overwhelming to ordinary minds. They display a rare kind of fortitude in the face of danger and opposition and often are inspired by them. To them, their ideals override any other consideration appertaining to normal life.

Totally immersed are they in their ideals that anything else is trivial. They endure a kind of loneliness only their rare class understands. Subject are they to ridicule, admiration and abuse on a scale matched only by their rare deeds.

To this world of rare breeds, Marcus Moziah Garvey belonged. His place confirmed by his rare deeds. Perhaps not a giant during his life time, but one whose name has been sealed in history among the greats, by subsequent events in Africa and further afield.

Garvey was universally known to the whole world at the prime of his career. At the height of his power, he inspired millions of black men and women the world all over. He also angered many. He possessed all the qualities that go into making a great leader. His kindness and understanding knew no bounds; his ability to grasp other peoples' problems was without an equal; he was full of passion and zeal; he cared less how he lived and more how others did; as an orator, he swayed the hearts and minds of millions; as a statesman, he simply had no equal and was in a class of his own, and perhaps his greatest gifts were insight, an ingenious mind, and great personal charisma.

And yet this strange mixture of a man was equally humble. He never spoke ill of his enemies and always answered back to criticisms with a characteristic charm and wit. He never was, or, ever claimed to be, a paragon of virtue. Hounded by his enemies both black and white, Garvey was supplied with the most lethal ammunitions to carry on the struggle to liberate fellow black man. The more he was criticized and opposed, the more he was inspired to carry on.

Marcus Garvey was also easily the most controversial figure of his time. He was also, perhaps, the greatest hope for all African peoples that has ever walked the earth. Certainly no one else in the history of African peoples did as much to inspire his fellow men and women as did Marcus Moziah Garvey. That he was controversial is probably not surprising. His program of uniting all African peoples of the world under one country and government in Africa was itself controversial enough.

Nobody had attempted it before, and it took the great mind and personality of Garvey to contemplate the idea in the first place. He took on the might of the white world and single-handedly challenged the so-called notion of white supremacy. He tirelessly strove to restore lost dignity and hope in the African. He gave birth to "African Nationalism" and gave this notion true meaning as no other African had done in modern history.

In his time, Garvey was hated and loved, admired and criticized, ridiculed and praised, understood and mis-understood, and called a saint and a devil. And yet ridiculed, hated, and criticized as he was, years after his lamentable death, what he said and predicted has been borne out to the letter.

> The African is still in chains both home and abroad

Among the African Americans, Garvey's main critics were the so-called intellectuals 'pseudo-intellectuals' to be precise. They saw nothing good in Garvey and the fact that he had not been favored with high academic learning, was therefore unfit to lead the race. But unlike most of them, this "ill-educated" dreamer knew the true history of his ancestors.

Indeed, Garvey was what he was, because he knew so well Africa's glorious past.

There have been arguments as to how Garvey (with nothing written of the glorious past of the Africans), knew so much about the African's past greatness. His critics simply dismissed him as a mad dreamer! But how did he know? One explanation is possible:

Garvey's father was a direct descendant from the Maroons as we have seen in the previous chapter. The maroons had never relinquished their Africaness. They had carried all their stories about their glorious past well stored away in their heads up to the plantations.

It is therefore possible that young Garvey's father passed on to him these stories which he himself had picked up from his stubborn parents. This knowledge of his ancestor's past had stood Garvey in good stead to argue and agitate uncompromisingly for the African peoples' freedom and self-determination all over the world.

Garvey is best known for his "Back to Africa" and "Africa for the Africans" philosophies espoused by him at the height of his career. These philosophies by Garvey were at best misunderstood, and at worst interpreted out of proportion by his critics, both white and black. He was even dubbed a racist! But was he? A realist—yes; a racist—never!

Garvey, felt more than anybody else at the time, strong indignation against the way in which African peoples were treated all over the world. He was convinced through his travels in the West Indies, Central and South America, and Europe that the only hope for the African person lay exclusively in the ability to re-group, organize, and aggressively seek to be self-reliant, self-governing and free again in the land of his ancestors.

In a way, Garvey lived in two totally different worlds at the same time. He lived first in the world of his ancestors back in Africa, as men of affairs, great rulers, inventors, and creators, free and independent. He also lived in a world with his people robbed of their freedom, and dignity, without power and influence, and treated as sub-humans in captivity and chains. For Garvey, with his unique comprehensive mind, something radical had to happen if the black man was ever going to regain his freedom and dignity in this world.

That Garvey should have addressed himself to the entire African world is perhaps not too surprising. Ever the realist that he was, he knew that until all African men and women of the world were free, not a single one could claim real freedom and independence.

In an impassioned plea to the conscience of all African peoples, he said, "The African needs a nation and a country of his own, where he can best show evidence of his own ability in the art of human progress. Scattering him as an unmixed and unrecognized part of alien nations and civilizations is but to demonstrate his imbecility, and point him out as an unworthy derelict, fit neither for the society of Greek, Jew nor Gentile. It is unfortunate that we should so drift apart, as a race, as not to see that we are but perpetuating our own sorrow and disgrace in failing to appreciate the first requisite of all peoples— *organization.*"

"No African," he went on, "let him be American, European or West Indian, shall be truly respected until the race as a whole has re-emancipated himself, through self-achievement and progress, and from universal prejudice. The African will have to build his own government, industry, art, science, literature and culture, before the world will stop to consider him. Until then, we are but wards of superior race and civilization, and outcasts of a standard social system."

"The race needs workers at this time, not plagiarists, copyists, and mere imitators, but men and women who are able to create, to originate and improve, and thus make an independent racial contribution to the world civil ization."

*   *   *

It's quite conceivable that some of the things Garvey said, may have been what one would call, rhetoric. But it has to be pointed out that this was quite a fraction compared to the huge sense he made in what he said on a number of occasions. The rhetorical bit of it may have been part of Garvey's tactic of hammering home the point!

After all, when one is engaged in the mobilization and rescue of over 400 million peoples scattered all over the world, using rhetoric to appeal to them is quite inevitable. This has to be distinguished from preaching or telling carefully planned lies which was charged of Garvey.

To the ordinary African person in the West Indies, Europe, the Americas, and Africa, Garvey was welcome news! He spoke their language, understood their desperate position, and reflected their impatience and indignation against the oppressive system they were compelled to live under. Above all, he saw their hitherto unserved interests as paramount and was determined, heavens come down, hell let loose, that those interests should be served.

To the so-called black elite, however, Garvey was bad

news! He was seen as a threat, as a trouble maker, un-representative of their interests, and as a champion of doom. With carefully planned propaganda by whites depicting Africa as a 'dark' continent, the last thing the so-called black intellectuals were prepared to entertain was Garvey's idea of "going back home to the land of their ancestors to build and create their own." They preferred instead to stay and fight for *equality* with the white man in his land. What they sadly failed to realize was that this same 'dark'continent, was also blessed with wealth on a scale the kind of which was hard to compare. The main beneficiary not being the African, the owner, but the white man, the aggressor and exploiter!

Garvey saw the African race in complete disarray, vul-nerable, without proper leadership and any sense of purpose about it at all. No meaningful program to date had been formulated to advance the cause of the development of the black world. The white world was unprepared to concede the most basic rights to the black world. Both the military and economic positions of the white world were advancing at a rate the African world could never hope to catch up with.

To Garvey, the exploitation and the suppression of the black man by the white man was there to stay, unless and until a radical programme was instituted forthwith to remedy the situation. Against this background Garvey, almost single handedly, set upon the tough road to change the shape of the world, to give fellow Africans a chance.

He desperately wanted to see a world in which African peoples played their humble part as free people, as thinkers, creators, inventors, and above all, as masters of their own destiny in their own land, as they had done for centuries before.

THE U.A.I.A.

The *Universal African Improvement Association,* started by Garvey in the summer of 1914, was exactly what it stated. It was universal, in order that it may embrace every African in the world; it was primarily for the task of improving the lot of the suffering masses of the African peoples; and it had to be an association as the organizing body for African causes.

Immediately after arrival back in Jamaica, from his successful but at the same time saddening trip to Europe, Garvey, highly inspired, set upon putting into motion the wheels of this great body. On establishing it, he invited all the African peoples or "persons of African parentage" to join hands with him and together, mobilize all the African peoples of the world into one strong body of government and country.

At a hastily called meeting, Garvey himself was elected President and Travelling Commissioner of the new organization. Thomas Smikle, was elected vice president to Garvey; Eva Aldred, was elected President of the Ladies Division; T.A. McCormack, was elected General Secretary; and Amy Ashwood, as Associate Secretary. Amy Ashwood, later became Garvey's first wife although the marriage turned out to be a "mismatch" ending in divorce after only three months.

The Headquarters of the organization, were set at; 30

Charles Street, Kingston.

For Garvey, his greatest dream of uniting all African peoples of the world through an organization, had at last been realized. Equipped as he was with determination, dedication and power of persuasion, it would be a matter of time before millions of African men and women would flock to enlist in the new organization. Despite early set-backs, Garvey is reputed to have organized more people and raised more money for African causes than any other man in African history. The humble beginnings of it all were in his native Jamaica!

*   *   *

The aims and objectives of the U.A.I.A. were to be:

"To establish a Universal Confraternity among the race; to promote the spirit of pride and love; to reclaim the fallen; to administer to and assist the needy; to assist in the development of independent African nations and communities; to establish a central nation for the race where they will be given the opportunity to develop themselves; to establish commissaries and agencies in the principal cities of the world for the representation of all Africans; to promote a conscientious spiritual worship among peoples of Africa; to establish universities, colleges, academies and schools for racial education and culture of the people; to improve the general conditions of Africans everywhere."

It was unanimously agreed that the motto of the organization should be: *One God! One aim! One destiny!* To this Garvey wrote the preamble which read:

"The Universal African Improvement Association and

African Communities League is a social, friendly, humanitarian, charitable, educational, institutional, constructive, and expansive society, and is founded by persons desiring to the utmost, to work for the general uplift of the African peoples of the world. And the members pledge themselves to do all in their power to conserve the rights of their noble race, and to respect the rights of all mankind, believing always in the Brotherhood of Man and the Fatherhood of God." He went on, "Therefore, let justice be done to all humankind realizing that if the strong oppresses the weak, confusion and discontent will ever mark the path of man, but with love, faith, and charity towards all, the reign of peace and plenty will be heralded into the world and the generations of men shall be called blessed."

All set to go, Garvey did everything humanly possible to promote the new organization among African peoples.

Passionately he said of the new body, "The U.A.I.A. teaches our race self-help and self-reliance, not only in one essential, but in all those things which contribute to human happiness and well being. The disposition of the many to depend upon the other races for a kindly and sympathetic consideration of their needs without making the effort to do for themselves, has been the race's standing disgrace, by which we have been judged, and through which we have created the strongest prejudice against ourselves."

*   *   *

In spite of such impassioned speeches, Garvey was soon to encounter rather unexpected problems as he tried to promote the new organization to the African West Indians.

Until he got into the 'thick' of things, Garvey wasn't aware of how much colour prejudice there was in his native Jamaica. The Mulatoes (people of mixed race), on one hand felt sufficiently threatened because they thought Garvey was too "dark" in complexion to lead them. The black elite, on the other hand, felt he wasn't 'educated' enough to be looked upon as a race leader. The poor, were simply too pathetic and years of oppression and poverty had reduced them to an embittered mistrusting lot!

Even those as dark as Garvey was, and even more so who had believed themselves white, opposed him. The white press, as well, did everything possible to discredit Garvey. He was called crazy; to use openly the term "Negro" and yet everyone beneath his breath was calling the African, a nigger!

Garvey soon found that he had to decide whether to please his so-called friends and be one of the 'black-whites' of Jamaica and be reasonably prosperous, or come out openly, and defend the integrity of the African world, and suffer for it. Characteristically, he opted for the latter hence his cardinal crime against the 'colored-black-white' society.

In spite of this stiff opposition, Garvey spent hundreds of dollars of his life savings helping the organization to gain a footing. He also dedicated all his time to the promotion of its ideals, consequently becoming a marked man, but was determined come what may that the work should be done.

In one sense, the First European War last century, turned out to be a blessing in disguise for Garvey. It did a great deal in arousing the consciousness of the African people to the reasonableness of Garvey's program, especially after the British wouldn't entertain the idea of West Indian Africans becoming officers in the British Army.

The fact that Africans had fought and died for 'democracy,' didn't impress the British one single bit. But it left the Africans feeling bitter! Who would blame them?

Garvey, succeeded to a greater extent in establishing the association in Jamaica, thanks largely due to help of a Catholic Bishop; the governor at the time, Sir John Pringle; Rev. William Graham, a Scottish clergyman; and several white 'friends.'

It is ironic that these gentlemen should have showed such enthusiasm for Garvey's controversial program in the first place. They did so, one cynically supposes, not really because they were genuinely interested in the re-emancipation of the African as such, but because they believed that the program would at least help rid Jamaica and the other white world of the African; especially the so-called black elite who were striving to be on the same footing with the white man in his land!

*　　　　　*　　　　　*

At this time, Garvey, was in close contact with Booker T. Washigton, the sage of Tuskegee Institute in Alabama. He wrote to Garvey encouraging him in his work for the U.A.I.A. and invited him to come over to America promising to go speaking with him. Unfortunately for Garvey, Washington died during the fall of 1915, before Garvey was ready to go to America. This untimely death of Washington, created a leadership vacuum among the

African Americans which Garvey would soon fill. With the organization now off the ground, Garvey started looking farther afield.

On March 23, 1916, barely a year after Washington's death, Garvey with his head spinning with ideas, arrived in Harlem, New York, to set up branches of the U.A.I.A. under African American leadership.

Marcus Garvey's grave in Hero's Park in Kingston, Jamaica. The author paying his respects.

This inscription reads:"We declare to the world Africa must be free." Statement made by Marcus Garvey in 1915.

7

Marcus Garvey
...in the U.S.A. & His Vision of Africa

Initially, Garvey had no intentions of staying in the U.S.A. at all. All he had wanted to do was to establish branches of the U.A.I.A. there and promote it to the African Americans in America. He wanted to hurry back to Jamaica and set up a trade college along the lines of the Tuskegee Institute started by Booker T. Washington.

Such an institution, Garvey hoped, would give Africans in Jamaica the opportunity not only to learn a trade but also to produce competent men and women as technicians to be sent to Africa to help out with development aspects.

He also intended setting up an African cultural centre to supplement the institute. This was meant to re-educate the Africans in the West Indies and the entire Western world in the ways of Africa, the home of their ancestors. After all, according to Garvey, they would all one day return there!

But it was not to be! The call for service and leadership in America was far greater than Garvey could resist. There was also the need for someone to take over from whence Booker T. Washington left off. The African masses were disillusioned and openly yearning for true leadership and the climate was ripe for a program which for once addressed itself exclusively to black issues.

Garvey could not have chosen a better time to arrive in America! The spiritual need among the African Americans was in abundance and, a *Messiah*, the African Moses had arrived!

When Garvey set upon establishing his organization in America, however, he soon realized that there were among African Americans two distinctive schools of thought both bitterly opposed to each other. One was espoused by Booker T. Washington and the other by Dr. W.E.B. Dubois.

Washington summed up his philosophy in his celebrated "Atlanta Compromise" address of 1895 when he told his African audience, "Do not antagonize the white majority. Do not ask for the right to vote. Do not fight for civil liberties or against segregation. Go to school. Work hard. Save money. Buy property. Some day, the other things may come." Washington may have been a bit too optimistic—or possibly naive.

Dubois on the other hand, argued that the African Americans would suffer permanent handicap socially and economically, if they held back from seeking full equality with the whites. With the help of leading Africans and some liberal whites, Dubois had formed the National Association for the Advancement of Coloured People (N.A.A.C.P.) in 1909.

Garvey, now active on the scene, openly ridiculed the N.A.A.C.P. as a reactionary organization and one which would add to, rather that solve, the African's problems.

This overt criticism of Dubois and his organization, though well intended, set both men at each others throats for a long time to come. Dubois represented the African elite on one hand and Garvey the workers on the other.

So it was the U.A.I.A. led by Garvey in the red, black and green corner (the colors of the U.A.I.A. flag) and the N.A.A.C.P. led by Dubois in the white corner. The tragedy was that half way through the fight, Dubois and his men took off their gloves and it became a bare knuckle fight by them to the finish! The African struggle movement was dealt a devastating blow! A blow it would take long to recover from.

W.E.B. DUBOIS

W. E. Burghardt Dubois was born in Great Barrington, Massachusetts in 1868. As both his last two names reveal, he was of mixed parentage. One part of him was Dutch, one part was French, and the other African. In Jamaican race terminology, he was a Mulatto. In American race distinction, he was coloured. Thus, unlike his arch enemy Garvey, he was light skinned and nearer to white than African. From the word go, Dubois had lost no time in impressing upon Africans of unmixed stock the "superiority" of coloureds over them.

As a boy, some wealthy whites assisted him financially in his education. Being academically inclined, he worked hard winning a place at Harvard University and later graduating with a Doctor of Philosophy.

So with a privileged background, better academic credentials, and a light complexion, Dubois saw himself as the heir apparent to Booker T. Washington and as the chief spokesman for all Africans in America.

To Dubois, Garvey was "too dark and too ill educated to lead the race!" Once in a derogatory fashion, he referred to Garvey as a "little fat black man, ugly, but with intelligent eyes, and a big head," in an article in the February 1922 issue of *Century Magazine*. Garvey, not to be out done, replied wittily, "According to the racial beauty standard of white people, this is a disparaging reference used to ridicule a man but as it comes from the pen of a colored man, it is he who looks ridiculous for he belongs to a race whose standard of beauty must be measured by the likeness of its majority. Therefore, 'black' is the logical reference besides, 'colored' suggests adulteration— displeasing to equatorial Africans." He went on, "Dr. Dubois ought to know that the standard of beauty within a race is not arrived at by comparison with another race, as for instance, if we were to desire to find out the standard of beauty among the Japanese people we would not judge them from the Anglo-Saxon viewpoint but from the Japanese." He concluded, "Therefore, if there is any ugliness in the African race it would be reflected more through Dubois than Marcus Garvey, in that he himself tells us that he's a little Dutch, a little African."

So Garvey's arrival in America, in effect, marked the arrival of the third school of thought. Garvey was totally opposed to the idea of African Americans seeking equality with whites for no other reason than that he was convinced the whites would never, *never* give in on this one.

Also, his arrival on the scene as if pre-determined, coincided with a wave of racial violence against African Americans across America.

It was in September, 1917, after clashes between African soldiers and civilians in Houston, Texas, that thirteen African Americans without proper trial were hastily sent to the gallows; forty-one of their white mates were first sentenced to life imprisonment but were later pardoned amid great African public outcry. Within the same year, 1917, East St.Louis witnessed ugly race riots which left forty African American men dead. Two years later in 1919, no less than twenty-six race riots took place across America.

A year before Garvey's arrival, the Ku-Klux-Klan had reemerged on the scene in great strength and was by this time a force to be reckoned with. The lynching of African Americans was on the increase and every year saw more and more defenseless men and women mowed down with no steps taken by successive governments to contain the situation. This is the general situation which had greeted Garvey on arrival in the USA. Not one re-known for looking on with folded arms and doing nothing, Garvey set upon with more vigour and vitality to do something.

First, he set out to meet as many African American

leaders as he could to study them and to see the programmes, (if any) they had formulated to advance African causes.

He particularly wanted to know what steps they were
taking to counter racial violence against Africans. He
travelled the length and breadth of America on this fact
finding mission. He was soon bitterly disappointed!

Not only was there no real effective programme to
counteract the racial violence against African Americans,
but also the leaders at the time were mere opportunists
who were *in it* for what they could get *out of it* for
themselves, at the expense of the poor.

Garvey fell on America like thunderstorm. The news of
his arrival spread across America like fire on dry grass.
Everywhere he went, he was received and greeted by
hundreds of thousands of enthusiastic followers. His
magnetic personality magnetized even the most indolent
of the poor African Americans. His fiery speeches, like
never before, penetrated the inner most souls of African
masses within and without America. But they also angered the African elite and white conservatives who
opposed him vehemently. Soon they would be waging a
bitter campaign to have Garvey thrown out of America!

He established the first branch of the U.A.I.A.in
Harlem in 1917, and within months, the branch was
boasting a membership of 1,500 strong followers. "Wake
up you mighty race," he thundered in his appeal to African
Americans.

As he travelled around the country to promote the
work of the organization, he preached the notion of self-
reliance by African Americans. Said he, "No longer

must our race look to whites for guidance and leadership; who best can interpret the anguish and the needs of our people but an African?"

Of the organization he said, "This organization under God will thrive without the demoralizing effect of existing off the charity of whites." He went on, "Among the many things the race needed (and badly too), were self-respect and self-reliance. Henceforth they must think **for** themselves and *of* themselves, only relying on their **own** initiative and ability to right the wrongs done them."

In desperation, some African Americans had simply resorted to skin bleaching and hair straightening in order to look like whites, or in case of African men, married white women in order to 'improve' the complexion of their children; 'marry-up' was the slogan of the day among some African Americans.

Garvey passionately appealed to black newspaper publishers and their owners to stop carrying advertisements for skin-bleaching and hair straightening chemicals. This naturally angered businessmen as it *killed* their revenue!

In a direct challenge to African American men, he said, "Take down the pictures of white women from your walls. Elevate your own women to the place of honour. They are for the most part the burden bearers of the race. Mothers: give your children dolls that look like them to play with and cuddle. They will learn as they grow older to love and care for their own children and not neglect them. Men and women," he continued, "God made us as His perfect creation. He made no mistake when he made us African with kinky hair. It was a divine purpose for us to live in our natural habitat—the tropical zones of the earth.

Forget the white man's banter that God made us in the night and forgot to paint us white. That we were brought here against our will is just a natural process of the strong enslaving the weak. We have outgrown slavery but our minds are still enslaved to the thinking of the master race. Now take these kinks out of your mind instead of out of your hair. You are capable of all that is common to men of other races so let us start now to build big business, commerce, industry, and eventually a nation of our own to protect us wherever we choose to live."

He concluded, "A beggar-race can never be respected. Stop begging for jobs and create your own. Look around you and wherever you see the need for factories and business, supply it. Stop begging for a chance and make it yourself. Remember, God helps those who help themselves!"

As the now awakened African Americans realized the reasonableness of Garvey's program, they flocked in their hundreds of thousands to register in the new organization. For the first time in their living memory, African Americans were witnessing on a mass scale activities of an organization which promised hope long denied them! As the numbers swelled by the thousands, it became necessary to start up branches of the U.A.I.A. all over America and beyond.

About the same time, Garvey saw the need for a newspaper as the chief organ of the organization. Therefore, in the early part of 1919, he published the first edition of the *Negro World.* As well as editing it, he also regularly contributed articles on the front page. In them, he passionately appealed to African men and women; wherever they may be, to seek to be self-reliant, self-respecting, and to re-group and go back to Africa (the land of their forefathers) and build a nation of their own.

The paper became an overnight success necessitating editions in Spanish and French languages to reach a wider readership. Front-page slogans were: "The indispensable weekly, the voice of the awakened African, reaching the masses everywhere."

The slogan **Africa for Africans**, preached through the paper by Garvey became a direct challenge and threat to white America resulting into the paper being labelled "seditious." Anybody found in possession of it was lashed and imprisoned. This however, did little to deter the now awakened and determined African American. In spite of risks involved, the paper was carried by trains, and ships and smuggled in all forms to reach eager readers.

Garvey himself meanwhile was unrepentant of his 'wicked' ways. According to him, stiff opposition from white America suggested he was doing something good for his suffering race. He supplemented the editorial page with an eight-point platform which read:

a.   *To champion African nationhood by redemption of Africa*

b.   *To make the African race conscious*

c.   *To breathe ideals of manhood and womanhood in every African*

d.   *To advocate self-determination*

e.   *To make the African world-conscious*

f.   *To print all the news that will be interesting and instructive to the African*

g.   *To instill racial self-help*

h.   *To inspire racial love and self-respect*

This open challenge quickly widened the scope of Garvey's enemies among both whites and African Americans alike. Soon he would be fighting for not only his own survival, but also that of the organization in America.

After hectic consultations among the members of the N.Y. branch, Garvey was formally invited to stay on in America, and at the same time, elected President General of the American branch of the U.A.I.A. Under his dynamic leadership, the organization grew by leaps and bounds. By June 1919, the organization had a full membership of 2,000,000 people. This was made possible by his writings and speeches across America. Like never before, the African American had been awakened never to go back to sleep. Like never before, he was no longer just statistics, but a full human being capable of the 'impossible.' Marcus Moziah Garvey, had seen to that! The African American like never before could now look forward to the dawn of happier days! But it was not to be.

His first public clash with white America was with one self-centred Edwin P. Kilroe, an Assistant District Attorney in New York.

Some African Americans obviously envious of Garvey's huge success and popularity across America, made unfounded allegations about Garvey and the U.A.I.A., to Kilroe. These foes of Garvey's were no more than failed politicians who were seeking cheap favors with white America and out to destroy Garvey. Kilroe responded swiftly by carrying out a series of investigations into the activities of the U.A.I.A. and its leadership.

Garvey was summoned to Kilroe's office no fewer than nine times to explain his real intentions in America and those of his now flourishing U.A.I.A. Obviously Kilroe relished the "god-given chance of giving a dressing down to nigger leader," and enjoyed it every time Garvey had come to his offices.

Garvey, true to his grit, got fed up with Kilroe's childish behaviour and wrote an article in the *Negro World* criticizing him. For this, he was sued for criminal libel, indicted and arrested. The case was subsequently dismissed when Garvey, rather than waste his precious time battling with one Kilroe in courts, retracted what he had written—for he knew he had better things to do and a greater need to serve!

But that was not the end of the whole affair! Kilroe, feeling vengeful, intensified his campaign to 'get' Garvey.

One day in the month of October 1919, Garvey was at his desk in his offices at 56 West 135th Street, New York City, doing his normal routine work. A man came inside the building and announced his name as Tyler and insisted he had to see Garvey urgently, upon which he was directed to Garvey's office and hurried up the stairs. On hearing the stamping on the staircase and someone shouting, "I want to see Garvey, I want to see Garvey!"

Garvey came out of his office and stood at the head of the stairs and in a kindly voice inquired: "You really want to see me?"

The man replied, "You Garvey? Well, I came to get you.

I've been sent by Mr. Kilroe!" Then he drew a 38-caliber revolver and started shooting at Garvey. He wounded him in his right leg and the right side of his scalp. Garvey fell to the ground and the would-be assassin believing Garvey to be dead, tried to run but was caught by the switchboard operator and others nearby. Garvey meantime was put in an ambulance and rushed to Harlem Hospital.

Tyler was arrested and taken in custody, pending "investigation" in the attempt on Garvey's life. Later it transpired that Tyler had confided to other inmates that he intended telling *all* when his case came up in court. On the day he was required to appear before a city magistrate however, Tyler was reported to have committed suicide by "jumping" from a second floor window, while being escorted by guards along a corridor. But when Tyler's body was later seen at the morgue by Garvey's aides, they reported that there was no evidence or signs of Tyler having fallen from a second floor window. There were no obvious injuries which were consistent with a fall from such a height!

When Garvey was out of the hospital and able to walk, his followers prevailed upon him to carry a gun for his own protection. Garvey characteristically replied: "I'm so lost in thoughts at times that I would not even remember I had the gun when I should use it. Using it is another question, I don't think I could kill anybody. As a boy I couldn't bear to see chickens killed, that is why I never eat them. When I see a chicken trussed up on the table, it reminds me of my people—innocent and carefree in the backyards of the world. Then suddenly some are pounced on, caught, and carried away to satisfy the greed of others."

He paused for a moment and then declared ecstatically; "No gun for me, if I'm to be killed then maybe it is my destiny."

The members however, fearing the blow the movement would be dealt should anything happen to Garvey, elected to have a bodyguard assigned to him. Marcellus Strong, his switchboard operator, was charged with the task of guarding him, and he also carried a gun.

THE BLACK STAR LINE COMPANY

The Black Star Line Company, as it was appropriately called, was one of Garvey's other bright ideas. He once said, "Just as there was a white star line, so there had to be a black star line." This idea, however, was first conceived after hearing reports of racial discrimination against African Americans in the maritime.

The idea was for the U.A.I.A. to acquire ships of its own which would be used exclusively for African development purposes; e.g. shipping raw materials and one day finished products from the West Indies and Africa and also according to Garvey's dream, "To carry all African men and women back to Africa to re-settle there!"

On June 27, 1919, the Black Star Line was incorporated and in the September of the same year, the U.A.I.A. acquired its first ship, the steamship *Yarmouth*. Garvey invited African American men and women through the *Negro World,* to buy shares in the company at five dollars a piece. Within months, Garvey had collected enough money to buy four more ships for the Black Star Line Company.

Practically all the employees of the Black Star Line Company were African and members of the U.A.I.A. The acquisition of ships added prestige to the U.A.I.A. as a body. White America looked on with sheer astonishment at the ability by one man to organize and do all that within a short space of time. He had come from humble Jamaica and had become famous. His name was now discussed on no less than five continents. He inspired confidence in the African masses as never before and stood out as a towering threat to 'white supremacy.' This was more than white and light skinned Americans could stomach. Trouble for Garvey was around the corner!

By August 1920, the U.A.I.A. was boasting a membership of 4,000,000 people. The U.A.I.A. was now a force to be reckoned with and Marcus Moziah Garvey, a five foot, stockily built *nigger* from the West Indies was bad news to white interests! He had to be stopped!

GARVEY AND THE KU KLUX KLAN

The story is told of the Jew who once went to the Ku Klux Klan offices. After being reminded by the attendants at the office that he should know better than to go there he replied, "But you don't understand, I'm here to see the guy who buys the white sheets!"

Garvey was dubbed by his African American enemies as a Klansman. The first African person in effect to hold this rather dubious distinction. Garvey never really embraced the Klan, rather the Klan embraced Garvey and his controversial program. The program (the first of its kind), won the Klan's sympathy and support because of what it sought to achieve.

Garvey, for totally different reasons from the Klan's, wanted African peoples to look to Africa rather than America as their ultimate home. In Africa, they would build their own and be masters in the land of their forefathers. In America, they were sure to remain second-class citizens all their life! Along these lines, Garvey talked about Africans looking to Africa.

The Klan's intentions then and now are to rid America of all African Americans purely on racial grounds. In Garvey, they readily found an ally who was helping them to achieve that end. Their limitless prejudices didn't allow them to see beyond an all-white America. The economic contribution African Americans have made and the vacuum it would create by their departure, were beyond the Klan's comprehension.

Ironically, Garvey might have survived the assassin's bullet during his stay in the U.S., precisely for not advocating equality with whites. That great liberal republican, President Abraham Lincoln, was gunned down for introducing reforms to help African Americans. Nearly a hundred years later, J.F. Kennedy was gunned down for showing sympathy with the plight of African Americans. His young brother, R.F. Kennedy for calling a spade a spade and "seeking a newer world" embracing Africans and other minorities. Finally, Martin L. King, Jr. for seeking equality with whites!

True, Garvey did visit the Klan's offices and met with the Imperial Wizard. But what better way to know what harm your enemy intends than by knowing the heart of that enemy?

AFRICAN PEOPLES CONVENTION

The African Peoples Convention called by Garvey in August, 1920, was the first of its kind in African history. Never before had so many African people gathered together to hear a fellow African speak.

They came from everywhere and all walks of life ; from America, the West Indies, Africa, and Europe and each had a story to relate about white domination and exploitation in their respective countries. It was by any standards a record breaking meeting. Garvey, without dispute, had been recognized as the leader.

The meeting in the evening was preceded by the parade during the day. All U.A.I.A. branches from all over America and beyond, smartly attired in their uniforms, marched in magnificent procession. In all, twelve bands provided the music and crowds lined the street sides to watch in sheer admiration.

The officials of the organization (Garvey included), rode in open carriages identified only by their streamers. The red, black, and green flags were everywhere to be seen. As the procession went on, the carnival atmosphere took over and bystanders, both black and white, happily joined in the festivities.

Later that evening in Madison Square Garden, before Garvey spoke to the crowds, the Universal Ethiopian Anthem was played and all the delegates joined in the singing.

The moment everybody had been waiting for arrived. The little Jamaican they had read about and heard so much about was about to address them live! To deafening applause, Garvey majestically rose to speak to them and said in his opening remarks: "We Africans are determined to suffer no longer. For over 500 years we have suffered at the hands of alien races. What is good for the white people is good for us."

"For democracy the nations of the world wasted Europe in blood for four years. They called upon the Africans of the world to fight. After the war, we were deprived of all of the democracy we fought for. In many instances in the Southern states, soldiers in uniforms returning from battlefields of Europe were beaten and a few lynched; before they were demobilized they were mobbed in this land of the brave. But we shall not give up. We shall raise the banner of democracy in Africa, or 400,000,000 of us will report to God the reason why."

"I know that America is the greatest democracy in the world, nevertheless, wherever I go, I am given to understand that I am an African. We pledge our blood to the battlefields of Africa where we will fight for true liberty, democracy and brotherhood of man."

"The African is not contemplating the initiating of the fighting, but we must protect ourselves and our interests. We are going in for mass organization. In the past we have worked separately and individually. Now we are going to organize."

"We are not," he went on, "distributing arms. We are not supplying implements of war." He concluded, "Preparing the African race mentally and physically, and the African will win out by evolution ..."

Garvey sat down to a thunderous applause; the clapping of hands, stamping of feet and knocking on tables went on for about five minutes ... They had come to listen to their leader, the messiah, the African Moses, and he had told them just what they wanted to hear ... Garvey now firmly fixed in his chair and greatly humbled by the response to his well-timed speech, could only look on appreciably. For once, he was lost for words!

"GOVERNMENT" IN EXILE

It hadn't occurred to Garvey quite what the delegates had in store for him. During the course of the conference (which in all lasted one month), the convention adopted the "Declaration of Rights of the African Peoples of the World." The convention also went on to form a government in exile and one day to take up power in Africa. To Garvey's great surprise, at only 33 years of age, he was unanimously elected Provincial President of United Africa and President General and Administrator of the U.A.I.A.

A cabinet of eighteen members was also elected and each member was assigned a department. After the colourful swearing in ceremony, Garvey, in his capacity as

Provincial President of Africa, conferred upon each
member either a peerage or knighthood such as, Duke of
the Nile. Others were made knights of the Distinguished
Service order of Ethiopia, Ashanti, and Mozambique.
They were from hence on to be smartly attired in robes
and caps. At the end of this uniquely successful meeting,
each delegate left vowing to do everything humanly possible to bring about a change ... a change to uplift the living
standards of the African throughout the world. For the
newly elected Provincial President of Africa though, it
was the beginning of endless battles with his enemies that
in the end resulted in his being thrown out of America!
A campaign for "Garvey must go" championed by the
likes of Dubois, was now hot.

THE COLLAPSE OF THE BLACK STAR LINE COMPANY

In the end, the collapse of the Black Star Line Company
was inevitable. Garvey's success and fame to some African
Americans (especially the light-skinned, so-called intellectuals), was more than they could tolerate. They started
carefully and maliciously planning his downfall. They laid
all kinds of traps for him to fall into. They saturated their
spies among the employees of the Black Star Line and
the U.A.I.A. His office records were stolen and were
never found. All of a sudden, employees started to be
openly dishonest and, even when tried and convicted, were
not sentenced and only dismissed by juries. Meanwhile,
the ships at sea were criminally damaged and there was a
general riot of wreck and ruin. Even the hitherto trusted

officers of the U.A.I.A, started to steal and be openly dishonest. When Garvey dismissed them as inevitably he had to, they joined the ranks of his now many enemies and had an endless fight on his hands to save the ideals of the association. For the Black Star Line Company the calamitous end came in December of 1921 due to increase in robberies both from within and without.

MARRIAGE TO AMY JACQUES

The collapse of the Black Star Line Company almost coincided with Garvey's breakup with his first wife, Amy Ashwood. The marriage had been in every sense a mismatch. Whereas Garvey preferred the indoor intellectual type of life and such company of people, his bride of five weeks enjoyed the 'casual ballet' type of life. Garvey found her not deep in thought at all and for a man committed to a cause embracing a record 400,000,000 peoples scattered all over the world, his companion had to take life a bit more seriously. The marriage ended in divorce in the sixth week!

Amy Jacques on the other hand turned out to be the perfect choice. With an intellectual background, more serious in thought and more concerned and sympathetic with the plight of fellow Africans, Garvey couldn't have wished for someone better!

She once made the *mistake* of going to listen to Garvey at Liberty Hall in N.Y., and was 'hooked' from then on. She was impressed most by his oratory and sincerity. After the meeting that evening, she went up to and spoke to Garvey about what he had said. Garvey obviously impressed and feeling 'hooked' himself, invited her to be his secretary and confidant. They fell in love and got married in July 1922, before Garvey's incarceration in the following year. Eight years later, she would bear a son named Marcus Garvey Jr. who became a lawyer. In 1932, they had a second son named Julius, presently a practicing medical doctor.

Amy Jacques, like Garvey, came from Jamaica. Her father lived in Cuba and Baltimore for a while and enjoyed travelling, and reading and spoke several languages. He went everywhere with his daughter on these trips and, at a young age, she had been exposed to the outside world. She had passed her Cambridge School Certificate Examination and won first prize and a place to study law. But her father thought otherwise. Said he, "I do not want my daughter to be exposed to the wiles of men in an office." But her exposure to the outside world led her to believe that she had to travel more and see, what if anything, she could do to help her less fortunate brethren. She travelled to Britain and finally settled in America. Both Britain and America exposed her to the plight of Africans. The meeting with Garvey could not have been more appropriate!

GARVEY ON TRIAL

The charge against Garvey, and his ultimate conviction, was nothing but racially and politically instigated. There was no shred of evidence to suggest that Garvey was in any way guilty of the crime he was supposed to have

Amy Jacques Garvey, isn't she beautiful!

committed.

Having failed to *get* Garvey any other way, his enemies resorted to the courts of 'justice' in order to destroy him and the organization. More the pity was the tragic fact that those leading the 'get Garvey' campaign were black men playing in the hands of the enemies of the race.

Garvey, and three other associates, were charged with using the mail to defraud in the course of their activities in the Black Star Line Company.

The case against Garvey and his co-defendants rested mainly on the assumption that they knowingly, and with criminal intent, used the mail to sell Black Star shares fully aware that the company was in financial ruins.

As the case unfolded before the court however, it became obvious that there was one man, and one man only on trial; and that was Marcus Moziah Garvey.

In a desperate attempt to gather as many "facts" as could be relied upon in order to secure a conviction, the prosecution took a whole year before it felt sufficiently confident to present a case against Garvey.

Meanwhile, in order to speed up Garvey's conviction and possible deportation, his arch enemies wrote to the United States Attorney General, Hon. Harry M. Doughty. In the letter, the eight signatories (all black or more appropriately light-skinned), maliciously gave reasons why the Attorney General as Chief Law Enforcement Officer, "Should use his full influence completely to disband and extirpate this vicious movement, (U.A.I.A.) and that he vigorously and speedily push the government's case against Marcus Garvey for using the mail to defraud ..."

They closed the letter by stating; "We sense the imminent menace of this insidious movement, which cancer-like, is gnawing at the vitals of peace and safety of civic harmony and inter-racial concord."

Against this background and in this hostile atmosphere, Garvey's trial began.

It was obvious from the word go that the trial of Garvey was just a legal 'formality.' As far as his enemies were concerned, he had been tried, convicted, and sent to jail long before he had taken the customary oath.

Garvey had picked, as his lawyer, an African American advocate by the name of Cornellius W. McDougald to defend him. The Honorable Judge JulianW. Mack was to preside over the case.

On the second day of the trial however, Garvey, fearing possible complicity by McDougald with the prosecution, dismissed him and elected to conduct his own defence.

On the same morning, soon after the proceedings started, Garvey made an application for his Honor Judge Mack to consider himself disqualified from the case. The grounds being that because of Judge Mack's membership of the N.A.A.C.P. (an organization vehemently opposed to Garvey) he would find it difficult to administer the same standards of fairness to the accused.

That the elementary principles of law had been violated by his appointment to try such a sensitive case. That as much as he, Garvey, respected the honour and integrity of the learned Judge, he nonetheless feared that in his trying his case and because of the circumstances involved, he would find it difficult not to be partial. A fair trial, therefore, would not be possible. "I therefore," he concluded, "respectfully submit that you, Judge Mack, remove yourself from trying the case and another judge be appointed in your place."

Judge Mack (obviously angered by this open challenge by a 'nigger') retorted that Garvey's arguments didn't hold water. That whereas he admitted being an active member of the N.A.A.C.P., he nonetheless would apply the same sense of 'fairness' in trying Garvey's case. The application was therefore rejected.

Garvey had made his point, but he had also made his own position very precarious! After this brief interruption, the trial resumed with Garvey now fighting for his life.

The prosecution wheeled in witness after witness to try to give some credibility to the case. One, Benny Dancy, had been paid to come forward and actually bear witness that Garvey, had caused promotional material to be sent through the post to him. On cross-examination by Garvey, however, Dancy frightened like a rabbit, testified that he had never received such matter. Is it any wonder that the whole case was 'fixed' in order to get Garvey?

At the end of it all, Garvey was found 'guilty' and sentenced to five years imprisonment and fined $1,000 plus court fees. Garvey tried to appeal against the sentence but to no avail. A white lawyer by the name of Armin Kohn, who handled his appeal, said of the case, "In my twenty-three years of practice at the New York Bar, I have never handled a case in which the defendant has been treated with such manifest unfairness and with such a palpable attempt at persecution as this one." What

Kohn said sums it up.

*   *   *

In 1927, when Garvey had nearly served the whole sentence, President Coolidge commuted it and, in December of the same year, Garvey (much to the jubilation of his enemies) was deported from the U.S.A. as an undesirable immigrant.

Before the *SS Salamance* which would carry him to Jamaica sailed off, Garvey addressed the huge crowd that had come to see him off. Passionately he told them, "The service to my race is an undying passion with me; the greater the persecution, the greater the desire to serve. Be not dismayed, Africa's sun is steadily and surely rising, and soon shall shed its rays around the world. I live and shall die for Africa redeemed. Steady yourselves and go forward!"

It was indeed an emotional occasion. As the ship slowly edged its way into the waters, the crowds now in tears started singing:-

Father of all creation,
Allah omnipotent,
Supreme O'er every nation,
God Bless our President.

Guide him thro' life victorious,
Save him from accident,
Grant him his aims most glorious,
God Bless our President.
The tyrant's wiles shall never,

Our homes asunder rent,
The Red, Black and Green forever,
God Bless our President.

One God! Our firm endeavor,
One Aim! Most glorious bent,
One Destiny! Forever,
God Bless our President.

Garvey, himself in tears, waved them finally and then retired to his cabin to ponder over his American adventure. Eleven years stay had taken him to the length and breadth of America, addressed endless meetings, met all kinds of people, angered many and, at the same time, inspired millions of African men and women to fight for freedom and justice!

He arrived in Jamaica to a tumultuous and emotionally rousing welcome, and after a short stay, he set sail for England. Here, he revived the U.A.I.A. and met many African students such as Jomo Kenyatta (later to become President of Kenya) and many others he was to inspire to return home and fight for *uhuru.** He died on June 10th, 1940 while still in England, from bronchial asthma. After independence, the Jamaican government exhumed his body and took it to Jamaica for a state burial in Heroes' Park. in Kingston.

* Kiswahili for Freedom

GARVEY'S INFLUENCE ON AFRICAN LEADERS

Five years after his death, The Fifth Pan African Congress under his influence took place in Manchester, England. The conference which was addressed by Kwame Nkrumah and was attended by Jomo Kenyatta, adopted Garvey's philosophy of *Africa for Africans* as its theme. The meeting, attended by Africans from other parts of the continent as well as West Indians, was to set in motion the wheels of the African freedom movement.

Soon afterwards, Jomo Kenyatta who was inspired by Garvey, returned to Kenya and was joined by the throng of other nationalists and political heavyweights such as Oginga Odinga, Tom Mboya, Daniel arap Moi, Bildad Kagia, Achieng Oneko, and Ronald Ngala, who were equally under the influence of Garvey to fight for *Uhuru*. The die-hards, such as the great Dedan Kimathi, were already a law unto themselves and were entrenched in the bush fighting for freedom. The dynamic, legendary Kwame Nkrumah followed suit and returned to the Gold Coast to stir up things there. Then Leopald Senghor returned to Senegal, and Boigny to Ivory Coast; within months the tide of freedom had swept across Africa like lightning!

Everywhere on the continent, the quest for freedom was now hot. The African, like never before, was determined the sky to come down, the oceans and seas to run dry, so that he should be free again. He was determined to be poor in freedom than rich in bondage. Garvey's influence had penetrated every nook and cranny of the

Rolihlahla Mandela

Kenneth Kaunda

Kambarange Nyerere

Robert Mugabe

Marcus Garvey

Joshua Nkomo

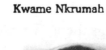

Kwame Nkrumah

Jomo Kenyatta

Bantu Biko

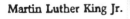

Martin Luther King Jr.

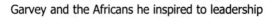

Garvey and the Africans he inspired to leadership

continent.

Everywhere the pot was equally boiling; Sekou Toure was stirring up things in Guinea, Patrice Lumumba in the Congo; Nyerere in Tanganyika; Obote in Uganda; Ben Bella in Algeria; Abubaker Tafawa Balewa; Namdi Azikiwe and company in Nigeria, Modibo Keita in Mali; and Albert Luthuli and Nelson Mandela in South Africa. Later Robert Mugabe, Joshua Nkomo, Ndabaningi Sithole, and company in Zimbabwe... Garvey's dream of seeing the continent free was on the verge of coming true at long last...

Tragically for Garvey, he was never to set foot on Africa soil. He had been banned from the colonies by the colonial powers. They feared his presence there would threaten their interests. Garvey, true to his reputation, was sure to cause some trouble for them!

But banned or not, his influence there was considerable; the legendary late King Sobhuza of Swaziland, is reported to have told Mrs. Garvey that he knew the names of only two African men in the Western World: Jack Johnson, the boxer who defeated the great white hope, Jim Jeffries, and Marcus Garvey. Much later, Kwame Nkrumah once admitted that, "I think that of all the literature that I studied, (while a student in the U.S.A.), the book that did more than any other to fire my enthusiasm was the *Philosophy and Opinions of Marcus Garvey.* He went on, "Long before many of us were even conscious of our own degradation, Marcus Garvey, fought for African national and racial equality."

Martin Luther King

Speaking at Garvey's shrine in Kingston in 1965, the late Civil Rights leader Dr. Martin Luther King said of Garvey, "...The first man in history on a mass scale and level to give millions of black people a sense of dignity and destiny and make the black person feel he was somebody."

Even his once arch-enemy Dubois, finally came to *his* senses and saw logic in what Garvey was striving to achieve for fellow Africans. It's interesting to contrast the following statements by the same learned Dr. Dubois about Garvey. In 1924, writing in his magazine *Crisis,* (the chief organ of the N.A.A.C.P.) He wrote, "The American Negroes have endured this wretch all too long with fine restraint, but the end has come. Every man who apologizes for, or defends Marcus Garvey from this day forth, writes himself down as unworthy of countenance of decent Americans. Garvey is without doubt, the most dangerous enemy of the Negro race in America and the world."

Sixteen years later after Garvey's lamentable death in London, the same Dubois (now awakened) said of Garvey and the U.A.I.A., "It was a grandiose and bombastic scheme, utterly impracticable as a whole, but it was sincere and had some practical features; and Garvey proved not only an astonishing popular leader, but a master of propaganda. Within a few years, news of his movement, of his promises and plans, reached Europe and Asia, and penetrated every corner of Africa."

Dubois did more than *a round about turn!* He responded to Garvey's call for Africans to prepare to go back to

Africa. He went and lived in Ghana, where he died in 1963.

One inevitably hastens to add that had eminent people such as Dubois, come to their senses earlier and joined hands with Garvey in the early days of his movement, the struggle might have assumed a different character altogether. But their support regrettably came when it was horribly too late...

Robert Minor, covering the 1924 U.A.I.A. convention for his paper the *Daily Worker*, said of Garvey in summary, "I heard Garvey speak last night. He is one of the most powerful personalities that I have ever seen on the platform. He is of the rare type that history finds rising in every unsettled period to express new currents among the masses of men. For weal or woe, Garvey is of the stuff that leaders (or every powerful misleader) are made of. Not the kind of leaders who rise in time of quiet and fit their environment as a fashion model fits the gowns of the day; but the kind of leaders that rise in times of storm and stress, who do not fit their environment, who look, feel and act out of place in the order of the day—who are called uncouth, who are jeered as misfits, and yet who may form the heads of the battering rams which smash down the walls of their environment." This sums up Garvey, the man, beautifully!

In eulogizing Garvey at the unveiling ceremony of his bust in Heroes' Park in Kingston in 1956, William Sherrill from the U.A.I.A. headquarters in New York, said in part: "Garvey was indeed a great man, and when we say great, we are not simply making a play on words. His greatness is proven by the standard which measures greatness.

Greatness is determined by the impact a man's work and teaching has on his times. When viewing the individual and his work, we ask ourselves—was the world different because he lived? The answer to this question as it relates to Marcus Garvey places him in the company of the great.

"Because Garvey lived, Jamaica is different; because Garvey lived, African America is different; because Garvey lived, Africa is different. His work and teaching gave birth to a new black man, a new Africa, and his impact went a long way in shaping a new world. For his cry was not alone 'Africa for Africans' but 'Asia for the Asiatic' and 'Europe for Europeans.' He did more to crystallize national sentiment in so-called backward countries than any single individual of our times. Measured by the standard of change, Garvey and his teachings have wrought in the world, Garvey rises to the heights of greatness.

"So great were the goals he set for his race that small minds criticized, and little men laughed, laughed as they always have at every new idea or venture. Some called him a fool. Others branded him a charlatan and buffoon; while the more charitable called him a dreamer. Too blind and shortsighted to realize the possibility of black men building for themselves, they sought to belittle his work by terming it a dream. Little did they realize that in calling Garvey a dreamer, they instantly placed him in the ranks of the greats.

"Dreamers! Do you know who dreamers are? They are the architects of greatness. Their vision lies within their souls. They peer through the clouds of doubt and darkness, and pierce the walls of unknown time.

"Dreamers! They sail seas that have never been charted,

because they are the makers of the charts. They scale mountains that have never been scaled, because they are the blazers of the way. They travel paths that have never been beaten, because dreamers are the beaters of the paths. Dreamers! The great American commonwealth was founded by dreamers; the world reforms that now benefit mankind were born in the hearts and minds of dreamers.

"Yes, Garvey was a dreamer, and because he dared to dream of a re-emancipated African race, a nationhood of African peoples of Jamaica are marching, black peoples of America are marching, and Africans are marching. The torch of freedom has been lighted in their breasts, and all the forces of hell cannot blow it out.

"We, from America, consider it a privilege and great honour to participate with the people of Jamaica in paying tribute to Marcus Garvey. His contribution to black America was no less than he made to his native land. I wish it were possible for me to do justice to the greatness of this son of Africa, but we cannot—words are inadequate!

"Bronze and stone too frail to convey a true picture of the man. For Marcus Garvey was one of history's providential geniuses. He came to his race endowed with an extraordinary ability for organization and leadership, as Shakespeare for poetry, Mozart for music, or Angelo for art. His undaunted faith in the possibilities of his people and his courage to come forward and plead their cause under any condition and circumstances, uniquely fitted him for leadership of the Universal African Improvement Association—an organization which has been an eternal blessing to his race and given immortal fame to his name.

"You, the people of Jamaica, knew him; you worked with him; some of you fought with him; you knew his strength and his weaknesses. But no man is perfect, what ever Garvey's faults, whatever Garvey's mistakes, let us now cover them with the pure mantle of love and tolerance for an otherwise great and noble character.

"Nothing we say can add or take away from the stature of Marcus Garvey. The world will soon forget what we say today, but it will long remember what he did. His name has a fixed place in history. As long as African men cherish the ideals of freedom and independence, Marcus Garvey's name will live in the hearts of his people everywhere ..."

IN RETROSPECT

In retrospect, Garvey did succeed in his venture, if one may so call it. His unique success has to be measured against opposition to him and all that he was trying to achieve for African peoples... and at the time that he tried to change things.

He dared challenge 'white supremacy' at the time it was thought unthinkable! He succeeded in teaching African people not to be ashamed of their colour. Nobody had done so with such vigour and eloquence before. He taught them to respect it and feel proud of it. He passionately appealed to African men to respect their women folk and not aspire to marry white women as a way of *moving up* the social ladder. He pleaded with African mothers not to be ashamed of buying black dolls (which he helped to manufacture) for their children. That yes, black, just like any other colour is **beautiful** and divinely bestowed upon African people. When the whole world had made being African a crime, he sought to make it respectable!

That he was opposed is perhaps hardly surprising. The world (the white world), neither then nor now, is prepared for change. Garvey sought to change the world. The unfair world. In the end, he was a victim of circumstances he partly helped create... like other greats before him in history, he was ahead of his time. He wanted to see a world in which African people had an equal chance and share as hitherto have not. Justice for Garvey, meant African peoples not living off charity and handouts from white people, but African people being able to achieve and be self-reliant as they had once been. He never wanted to see a world in which black ruled over, dominated, and exploited white, anymore than he could bear to see this imbalance in white favour. He desperately wanted to see his people, as men and women of affairs again, happily contributing to world civilization and stability as they had done centuries before.

He wanted to see the African man as a thinker, creator, inventor and master of his own destiny in his own land. Above all, he desperately wanted to see Africa free again, in every sense of the word. For he knew very well that until Africa and the Africans were free again, no African man or woman, wherever he or she may be, could be respected.

His writings, as we have seen, like no other written literature, helped inspire the fight for independence on the continent of Africa and beyond, and the struggle for civil liberties in America. That is no small achievement by any standards.

That Garvey lived and dared to question things, God blessed America with Martin Luther King Jr., and Malcolm X that they could carry on the struggle for civil liberties for fellow Africans and to free the white man from the captivity of his prejudices, that Garvey lived and dared to challenge 'white supremacy' God blessed Africa with Kwame Nkrumah, Jomo Kenyatta, and others to struggle to liberate mother Africa.

But the greatest of all his achievements, were his teachings which surpassed any other and helped to instill the notion of self respect and dignity in the African peoples ... then, they could believe in themselves again.

8

Marcus Garvey:
...Quotations

I thought it would be fitting to include a chapter on Garvey's *Philosophy And Opinions*. This was done for two reasons:

1) to let Garvey speak for himself, and

2) to enable the reader to make an independent judgment about Garvey.

A race without authority and power, is a race without respect.

Chance, has never yet satisfied the hope of a suffering people. Action, self-reliance, and the vision of self and the future have been the only means by which the oppressed have seen and realized the light of their own freedom.

There is nothing in the world common to man, that man cannot do.

The ends you serve that are selfish will take you no further than yourself, but the ends you serve that are for all, common, will take you even into eternity.

This is the day of racial activity, when each and every group of this human family must exercise its own initiative and influence in its own protection, therefore, African peoples should be more determined today than they have ever been, because the mighty forces of the world are operating against non organized groups of peoples, who are not ambitious enough to protect their own interests.

Wake up Africa! Let us work towards the one glorious end of a free redeemed and mighty nation. Let Africa be a bright star among the constellation of nations.

The political re-adjustment of the world means that those who are not sufficiently able, not sufficiently prepared, will be at the mercy of the organized classes for another one or two hundred years.

*The only protection against **injustice** in man is **power**— physical, financial, and scientific.*

The masses make the nation and the race. If the masses are illiterate, that is the judgement passed on the race by those who are critical of its existence.

Education is the medium by which a people are prepared for the creation of their own particular civilization, and the advancement and glory of their own race.

Nationhood is the only means by which modern civilization can completely protect itself. Independence of nationality, independence of government, is the means of protecting not only the individual, but the group. Nationhood is the highest ideal of all peoples.

The evolutionary scale that weighs nations and races, balances alike for peoples; hence we feel sure that some day the balance will register a change for the African.

The whole world is run on bluff. No race, no nation, no man has any divine right to take advantage of others. Why allow the other fellow to bluff you? Every student of political science, every student of economics knows that the race can only be saved through a solid industrial foundation. That the race can only be saved through political independence. Take away industry from a race; take away political freedom from a race, and you have a group of slaves.

Peoples everywhere are travelling towards industrial opportunities and greater political freedom. As a race oppressed, it is for us to prepare ourselves so that at anytime the great change in industrial freedom and political liberty comes about, we may be able to enter into the new era as partakers of the joys to be inherited.

Lagging behind in the van of civilization will not prove our higher abilities. Being subservient to the will and caprice of progressive races will not prove anything superior in us. Being satisfied to drink of the dregs from the cup of human progress will not demonstrate our fitness as a people to exist alongside of others, but when of our own initiative we strike out to build industries, governments, and ultimately empires, then and only then will we as a race prove to our Creator, and to man in general, that we are fit to survive and capable of shaping our destiny.

Let Africa be our guiding star—our star of destiny!

So many of us find excuses to get out of the black race, because we are led to believe that the race is unworthy— that it has not accomplished anything. Cowards that we are! It is we who are unworthy because we are not contributing to the uplift and up-building of this noble race.

How dare anyone tell us that Africa cannot be redeemed, when we have 400,000,000 men and women with warm blood coursing through their veins? The power that holds Africa is not Divine. The power that holds Africa is human, and it is recognized that whatsoever man has done, man can do.

We of the African race are moving from one state of organization to another, and we shall so continue until we have thoroughly lifted ourselves into the organization of government.

Be as proud of your race today as our fathers were in the days of yore. We have a beautiful history, and we shall create another in the future that will astonish the world.

Men who are in earnest are not afraid of consequences.

No one knows when the hour of Africa's redemption cometh. It is in the wind. It is coming. One day like a storm, it will be here. When that day comes, all Africa will stand together.

I pray to God that we shall never use our physical prowess to oppress the human race, but we will use our strength— physically, morally and otherwise to preserve humanity and civilization.

For over three hundred years, the white man has been our oppressor, and he naturally is not going to liberate us to the higher freedom—the truer liberty, the truer democracy. We have to liberate ourselves.

Every man has a right to his own opinion. Every race has a right to its own action: therefore, let no man persuade you against your will, let no other race influence you against your own.

The world ought to know that it could not keep 400,000,000 Africans down forever. There is always a turning point in the destiny of every race, every nation, of all peoples, and we have come now to the turning point of Africans, where

212 *No More Lies About Africa*

we have changed from the old cringing weakling, and transformed into full-grown men, demanding our portion as **men**.

Leadership means everything; **pain, blood, death!**

All peoples are struggling to blast a way through the industrial monopoly of races and nations, but the African person has failed to grasp its true significance and seems to delight in filling only that place created for him by the white man.

The African who lives on the patronage of philanthropists is the most dangerous member of our society, because he is willing to turn back the clock of progress when his benefactors ask him so to do.

No race in the world is so just as to give others, for the asking, a square deal in things economic, political, and social.

The greatest weapon used against the African is **disorganization**.

At no time within the last five hundred years can one point to a single instance of Africans as race of haters. The African has loved even under severest punishment. In slavery the African loved his 'master.' He safeguarded his home even when he further planned to enslave him. We are not a race of haters, but lovers of humanity's cause.

*We are living in a strenuous, active age, when men see, not through the spectacles of sympathy, but demand that each and every one measures up in proportion to the world's demand for service. The attitude of the white race is to subjugate, to exploit, and if necessary, exterminate the weaker peoples with whom they came in contact. They subjugate first, if the weaker peoples will stand for it: then exploit, and if they will not stand for **subjugation** or **exploitation**, the other recourse is **extermination**.*

There can be no peace among men and nations, so long as the strong continue to oppress the weak, so long as injustice is done to other peoples, just so long will we have cause for war, and make a lasting peace an impossibility.

Hungry men have no respect for law, authority, or human life.

I am not opposed to the white race as charged by my enemies. I have no time to hate anyone. All my time is devoted to the up-building and development of the African race.

The world does not count races and nations that have nothing. Point me to a weak nation, and I will show you a people, oppressed, abused, and taken advantage of by others.

Show me a weak race, and I will show you a people reduced to serfdom, peonage and slavery. Show me a well-organized nation, and I will show you a people and nation respected by the world.

The battles of the future, whether they be physical or mental, will be fought on scientific lines, and the race that is able to produce the highest scientific development, is the race that will ultimately rule.

*Let us in shaping our own destiny set before us the qualities of human **justice**, **love**, **charity**, **mercy, and equity**. Upon such foundation let us build a race and I feel that God who is Divine, the Almighty Creator of the world, shall forever bless this race of ours, and who to tell us that we shall not teach men the way of life, liberty, and true human happiness?*

All of us may not live to see the higher accomplishment of an African Empire—so strong and powerful, as to compel the respect of mankind, but we in our lifetime, can so work and act as to make the dream a possibility within another generation.

In the fight to reach the top, the oppressed have always been encumbered by the traitors of their own race, made up of little faith and those who are generally susceptible to bribery for the selling out of the rights of their own people. As Africans, we are not entirely free of such an encumbrance.

If Europe is for the white man, Asia is for the brown and

yellow man, then surely Africa is for the black man. The great white man has fought for the preservation of Europe, the great yellow and brown races are fighting for the preservation of Asia, and four hundred million Africans shall shed, if need be, the last drop of their blood for the redemption of Africa and the re-emancipation of the race everywhere.

I know no national boundary where the African is concerned. The whole world is my province until **Africa is free!**

God Almighty created us all to be free. That the African race became a race of captives was not the fault of God Almighty, the Divine Master, it was the fault of the race. Sloth, neglect, indifference caused us to be captives. Confidence, conviction, action will cause us to be free men again.

Where can we find in this race our real men? Men of character, men of purpose, men of confidence, men of faith, men who really know themselves? I have come across so many weaklings who profess to be leaders, and in the test I have found them but the captives of a nobler class. They perform the will of their masters without question.

The peace of the world cannot be settled by political conferences, or by industrial conferences only. If we are to have world peace, it will only come when a greater inter-racial conference is called; when Jew will meet Gentile, when Anglo-Saxon will meet Teuton, when the great Caucasian family will meet the Mongolian, and when all will meet the African, and then and there straigh-ten out the differences that have kept us apart for hundreds of years and will continue to keep us apart until Doom's Day, if something is not done to create better racial understanding.

A race that is solely dependent upon another for its economic existence sooner or later dies.

If the African were to live in this Western hemisphere for another five hundred years, he would still be outnum-bered by other races who are prejudiced against him. He cannot resort to the government for protection for govern-ment will be in the hands of the majority of the people who are prejudiced against him, hence for the African to depend on the ballot and his industrial progress alone, will be hopeless as it does not help him when he is lynched, burned, Jim-crowed, and segregated. The future of the African, there-fore, outside of Africa, spells ruin and disaster.

The time has come for those of us who have the vision of the future to inspire our people to closer kinship, to a closer love of self, because it is only through this appreciation of self will, that we will be able to raise to that higher life that will make us not an extinct race in the future, but a race of men fit to survive.

Men of the black race, let me say that a greater future is in store for us, we have no cause to lose hope, to become fainthearted. We must realize that upon ourselves depend our destiny, our future. We must carve out that future and that destiny.

Propaganda has been waged here, there and everywhere for the purpose of misinterpreting the intention of the Universal African Improvement Association; some have said that this organization seeks to create discord and discontent among the races; some say we are organized for the purpose of hating other people. Every sensible, sane, and honest-minded person knows that the U.A.I.A. has no such intention. We are organized for the absolute purpose of bettering our condition, industry, commercially, socially, religiously, and politically.

Prejudice is conditional on many reasons, and it is apparent that the African supplies, consciously or unconsciously, all the reasons by which the world seems to ignore and avoid him. No one cares for a leper, for lepers are infectious persons, and all are afraid of the disease, so, because the African keeps himself poor, helpless, and undemonstrative, it is natural also that no one wants to be of him or with him.

The disposition of the many to depend upon the other races for kindly and sympathetic consideration of their needs, without making the effort to do for themselves, has been the race's standing disgrace by which we have been judged and through which we have created the strongest prejudice against ourselves.

The African must be up and doing if he will break down the prejudice of the rest of the world. Prayer alone is not going to improve our condition, nor the policy of watchful waiting. We must strike out for ourselves in the course of material achievement, and by our own effort and energy, present to the world those forces by which the progress of man is judged.

The race needs workers at this time, not plagiarists, copyists and mere imitators; but men and women who are able to create, to originate and improve, thus make an independent racial contribution of the world civilization.

It is unfortunate that we should so drift apart, as a race, as not to see that are but perpetuating our own sorrow and disgrace in failing to appreciate the first requisite of all peoples—organization.

Gradually, we are approaching the time the African peoples of the world will have either to consciously, through their own organization, go forward to the point of destiny as laid out by themselves, or must sit quiescently and see themselves pushed back into the mire of economic serfdom, to be ultimately crushed by the grinding mill of exploitation and be exterminated ultimately by the strong hand of prejudice.

But when we come to consider the history of man, was not the African a power, was he not great once? Yes, honest students of history can recall the day when Egypt,

Ethiopia, and Timbuktu towered in their civilizations, towered above Europe, towered above Asia. When Europe was inhabited by a race of cannibals, a race of savages, naked men, heathens, and pagans, Africa was peopled with a race of cultured African men, who were masters in art, science, and literature; men who were cultured and refined; men who, it was said, were like gods. Even the great poets of old, sang in beautiful sonnets of the delight it afforded the gods to be in companionship with the Ethiopians.

My contribution to the race and to Africa is small, but it is gladly given without any regrets. Some of us will contribute through our ability and our lives, others through service of other kind; but whatever it be, let us give it freely.

There has never been a movement where the leader has not suffered for the cause, and not received the ingratitude of the people. I, like the rest, 'am prepared for the consequences.

After my enemies are satisfied, in life or death, I shall come back to you to serve as I have served before. In life, I shall be the same; in death, I shall be a terror to the foes of African liberty. If death has power, then count on me in death to be the real Marcus Garvey I would like to be. If I may come in an earthquake, or a cyclone, or plague, or pestilence, or as God would have me, then be assured that I shall never desert you and make your enemies triumph over you.

Would I not go to hell a million times for you? Would I

not, like Macbeth's ghost, walk the earth forever for you? Would I not cry forever before the footstool of the Lord Omnipotent for you? Would I not die a million deaths for you? Then, why be sad? Cheer up, and be assured that if it takes a million years, the sins of our enemies shall visit the millionth generation of those that hinder and oppress us. Remember that I have sworn by you and my God to serve to the end of all time, the wreck of matter and the crash of worlds...

Part Three

TOWARDS REAL FREEDOM

9

Hope For The Future

FREEDOM

Firstly, the very nature of the heading of this chapter pre-supposes that there is no real freedom for the African person at the moment.

Secondly, the absence of this freedom has to be as a result of certain deficiencies.

Thirdly, because there is no real freedom for the African person, the next logical question to ask is: what must be done to remove these deficiencies in order to attain real freedom?

But before any attempt is made to put forward possible solutions, it is necessary to define *freedom* in this context:-

WHAT THEN IS FREEDOM?

Freedom, first of all, is the complete human existence. It is the total unhindered expression of human values and attributes. It reflects the chemistry of the body as a whole in its functions, hence the freedom of speech, freedom from fear, freedom from want, and freedom to determine one's destiny. To deny any one of these is to deny real freedom, hence enslave the human race.

Now, having hopefully defined freedom as it should apply to the human race, let us now critically examine the positions of the African person inside and outside of Africa and see if they enjoy any of the freedoms described above.

But first, what are the independent positions of the African inside Africa and the African outside? What is the basic difference between the two? It is important to draw this distinction as it will help us to appreciate the overall position of the African person, whether home or abroad.

THE POSITION AND BASIC DIFFERENCE BETWEEN THE TWO AFRICANS

The African person outside Africa, is to certain extents, better off economically than the African person inside Africa. The African inside Africa is, to limited extents, better off politically. But both are principally not free. The reason being that neither enjoys all the freedoms described above.

THE AFRICAN PERSON OUTSIDE AFRICA

First, he is a minority as the case is in Europe and North America.

Secondly, his new country, though officially democratic, nonetheless, still resists his attempts to be an integral part of the society as a whole.

Thirdly, the obstacles (racially motivated) placed in his way, continually rob him of his inalienable right to function as a complete human being. Thus rendering him still an enslaved person, operating from the lonely banks of the main river housing all the wealth and comforts, he is blatantly denied.

Fourthly, though he is fully franchised, his participation in the political game, is only to serve those forces which perpetuate his underprivileged position.

Fifthly, as one who hails originally from the so called "dark continent" and a "primitive" heritage, he constantly has to grapple with the task impossible of proving to those who doubt him that he is nonetheless, not intellectually lacking or morally bankrupt as a result! This basically, is the position of the African person in the diaspora.

THE AFRICAN PERSON IN AFRICA

Firstly, although he is supposedly politically free, he is not economically so yet, as his economy is externally controlled.

Secondly, the colonial legacy has rendered him **dependent** hence, robbed him of the drive through self-initiative, to seek to be self-reliant and independent.

Thirdly, the colonially designed education system he has to go through, has everything about it, but a program of economic development for the continent.

Fourthly, the war situations (foreign induced), have denied him the peace and tranquillity conducive to development. I will go into detail about the four points later in the discussion. This, basically, is the position of the African in Africa.

So, we then come back to square one—the African per-son universally not being free in all the dimensions of the word.

WHY AND HOW FREEDOM HAS ELUDED THE AFRICAN WORLD

Inevitably, one has to address one's self to the question; why has freedom, hitherto, eluded the African world?

There are many who will argue that 'change ' is brought about by evolution; that things don't *happen* overnight; that the African will have to be *patient* and wait for his turn to be developed industrially, politically, and economically hence attain real freedom!

I don't subscribe to this thinking, as it is empty! Here, it is not a question of being patient or the lack of it. It is that the present state of the world economic order is such that industrial, political, economic, and social development for the African world is out of the question, like it or not. For the simple reason that in that order, nothing *provides* for the interests and the aspirations of the black world within and without Africa. In order to illustrate this point, let us look at the world set up.

THE WORLD ECONOMIC SET UP

The world, then, is divided up between two main groups; the first group consists of the so-called First world of the **haves** and the second group consists of the **have nots**. The first group of the **haves,** white controlled, own and control the means of production; whereas, the second group of the **have nots** largely African, only have their labor and raw materials to sell.

Now, in a highly technological world, such as we live in today, only those who own and control the **means** of production, can hope to survive. Of course there have been changes here and there geared towards 'giving' the black world a chance, but tragically, these changes are only cosmetic and don't offer real hope at any rate.

The gap, therefore, between the rich North and the exploited South, continues to grow bigger and bigger; hence the poor are getting poorer while the rich are getting richer, making nonsense of the idea of the *transfer* of some wealth from rich countries to poor ones. Infact, the gap is so big that there are only the **first** and the **exploited** worlds; no second world to fill in the gap! So one is either lucky and born white in affluent First world society or unfortunate and born black in poverty stricken and exploited South world society.

How the Economic Imbalance is Maintained by the Rich North

First, who are these lucky members of the First world? And who are the miserable unlucky members of the exploited world?

The First world mainly consists of the industrial giants such as Great Britain, North America, Germany, France, and now, our oriental friends, the Japanese.

I can safely say that the whole continent of Africa and South America and the West Indies, plus some parts of Asia, are at the moment permanent members of the Exploited World Body (EWB.) Now, the economic order is such that the exploited world countries supply vital raw materials to the industrial nations as we have seen above—what is wrong with that, one may ask?

Well, these raw materials are then *turned* into finished products to be sold back to the exploited world at exorbitant prices, having paid 'peanut' prices for the raw materials in the first place. A clever Dick might simply say; "Why can't these countries go industrial in order to compete adequately with the First world?"

The reason this can't happen (at least for the moment) is because of the richer nations' greed and their monopoly

The African growing coffee

Coffee as a finished product re-sold to the African at sky-high prices

of the world trade.

> With their superior technology, they are able to manipulate the trade and direct it in a direction favorable only to them at the expense of the **exploited** but **not** poor countries

RAW MATERIALS AGAINST FINISHED PRODUCTS

Here, I will address myself to a concrete example of how the First World exploits and consequently **under-develops** the already exploited South world.

We'll look at an exploited South country whose chief produce and export is coffee. We will imagine this exploited world country to be Uganda, and the First World country to be Britain. These two want to do business together purporting to benefit both at the close of the deal.

Uganda, starts off armed with several millions of coffee bags stacked in raw state in Mbale warehouses. Our friends, the British, start off in this intercourse, armed with several finished products e.g. agricultural machinery, the latest helicopter fighter bombers, a selection of automatic machine guns, vehicles and you name it, they have got it. And Uganda requires a number of these products for *development* purposes.

Let us imagine that Uganda wants to purchase from Britain, among other things, 10 helicopter fighter bombers. Each helicopter fighter costing about £ 200,000

Britain is paying Uganda for her *raw* coffee beans £1 per pound in weight. Uganda will need to turn over to Britain about 1667 bags of coffee before she can buy one helicopter fighter bomber.

But supposing Uganda sold to Britain coffee as a processed finished product, charging about £3 per pound in weight; she could expect to fetch from her 1,667 bags of coffee, about £600,000. So she would only need about 556 bags of coffee in order to purchase each helicopter fighter bomber from Britain, instead of the original 1,667 bags. Imagine, if you will, the difference!

This goes to say for other raw materials which our friends in industrial nations happily turn into finished products, and then re-sell to us at sky-high prices we can ill-afford... not to mention the fact that we then have to buy their currency first, in order to purchase these products as our currencies (Lord have mercy!), are not legal tender beyond our borders!

THE MYTH OF DEVELOPMENT

The example above of raw materials against finished products, may, to some, appear to be simple, but does, however, characterize the trade relationship between the rich North and the exploited South.

I now come to the question of development or the lack of it in the exploited world as a whole, and Africa in particular. The exploited countries (Africa included) are popularly referred to as 'developing countries' which in effect does imply that as developing countries, one day, they will be developed. This is a myth. There is no development as such taking place in these countries at the present moment. Why?

First, because the economies of most of these countries are agrarian and non-industry backed.

Second, the few sub-industries that they have been able to muster are inward looking producing inferior products for only local consumption and not for export.

Third, these few sub-industries depend heavily for day to day functioning, on foreign expertise often too expensive to maintain.

Fourth, most of these countries have got their priorities wrong, investing in non-productive and non-profitable ventures which only aggravate poverty in the end. Here are a few examples of what I'm talking about:

Let us take the example of Africa's embassies abroad. It costs on average about $150,000 to $200,000 (US) per month to maintain one mission and its staff abroad. This translates into about $2.4 million (hard currency), yearly to run a single embassy. Every African country maintains about forty missions abroad. This therefore translates into a bill of about $90 million (US) of public funds per African country to run missions abroad. Well and good so far.

But the next logical question to ask is how much money does each African country make from having diplomatic relations with other countries? Here, I'm talking in terms of trade. By how much does each African country profit out of these relations?

My reliable information through research reveals that hardly $10 million is made by any African country on the investment of the staggering figure of $90 million (US)

Now, don't get me wrong. I am not pretending to be an economist. But I don't think that one needs a Ph.D. in economics to know that this is bad business on part of African governments. If this is not squandering of public funds and impoverishing Africa, I do not know what it is!

*   *   *

Next example:

Sixty percent of the national budget in most African countries goes to purchasing arms from abroad for so-called national defence. Again here, I must confess that I am not a military expert, but I seriously doubt that any one single country in Africa, could hold up in a conventional war against any of the enthusiastic suppliers of these weapons. My research has revealed that most of the weapons Africa buys at exorbitant prices from abroad, are of inferior quality, incapable of fighting a conventional war! I consider most of the suppliers of these weapons to Africa as enemies of Africa. Now, tell me which enemy is *stupid enough* to supply you with weapons you could successfully turn against him? Tell me!

*   *   *

Next example:

I have made no secret of the fact that I am unhappy with the education system in Africa now, as it is misleading and under-develops Africa. Meaning that the wrong subjects are taught, or taught in such a way that at the end of an African's schooling, you end up with a half-baked Frenchman or Englishman with a black skin!

That's what education systems are producing in Africa.

Men and women who aspire to sit in offices attired in the best suits and dresses from Paris and London. Men and women who know more about the writings of Mr. William Shakespeare and the military adventures of Monsieur Napoleon Bonaparte, than all the English and French put together! Men and women who know nothing about Africa's glorious past. Men and women **ill-prepared** for the technological world we live in today. So all the monies poured into education in Africa today are good monies washing down the drain!

Please don't misunderstand me here! Let me put it another way. The education system in Africa should teach Africans (as their ancestors did before), to invent, create, manufacture, and sell things on world markets just as the Japanese, English, Americans, and Russians do! That's all I'm saying. Don't go around saying Nangoli is against education—because I'm not!

> All I'm against is the wrong type of education!

Furthermore, the education system Europe designed for Africa calls for higher intellectual standard than is necessary or is the case in the European education system itself. This system was meant for the African, to more than prove his intellectual worth in order to be *near* to a white man!

Africa today has more intellectuals going a round bombastically speaking French and English, as if the French and English really care. Intellectuals who are more proficient in these foreign languages than in their own mother tongue. Worst, the education system in Africa renders its students seekers of power for personal aggrandizement, rather than explorers of ideas for the advancement of society.

Take my own example: I failed the infamous Cambridge School Certificate Exam and was promptly declared academically unfit and intellectually *stupid* by the educational set up in my native Uganda. Today, I'm a university lecturer, author of the book you are reading and many others, largely due to the education I received from my father and grandfather, Chief Musamaali.

> But did I really fail?
> Or the questions were simply wrong and my answers were correct!
> To the question: What is the source of the Mississippi? I answered, Nalubaale (Victoria)! The correct question should have been: What is the source of Kyiira (Nile)?
> Asked to discuss Napoleon, I wisely discussed Mandela! What business did I have with a French man?

Let us carry on with the reasons for under-development in Africa:

Fifth, a state of war (often foreign induced) has been created in most areas in Africa hence denied the right kind of atmosphere to prevail to allow the exploitation of human resources for national development; look at Somalia, Liberia, Rwanda, Burundi, Congo, and former Zaire (now Democratic Republic of Congo) to mention a few!

Sixth, the natural resources of most of these countries,

are foreign exploited and *owned* resulting in the economies of these countries to be externally controlled.

Seventh, no advanced industrial sectors have been created to produce products to compete on international markets to boost national currencies, e.g., to enable these currencies to be internationally convertible hence remove the need and over-dependence on hard currency meaning principally the British sterling, the American dollar, the Deutch mark, the French and the Swiss francs, the Italian lira, and now believe me or not, the Japanese yen.

I say, *believe me or not,* in the case of Japan in a positive rather than negative sense. Only recently, as recent as the end of the Second European War (last century), Japan was just another poor country. But an industrial miracle has happened, and now, Japan is an industrial force to be reckoned with. Her national currency, heavily backed by industrial output, is now internationally convertible. It is in this light that I offer the seventh reason as contributory to under-development in Africa and the rest of the exploited world.

Now, back to my reasons for under-development ... *Eighth*, the multi-nationals based in industrial rich nations and their subsidiaries in the exploited world, dominate the world trade and ensure through unfair trade practices that only home economies benefit and those abroad are thoroughly exploited.

Ninth, political instabilities have made it almost impossible for meaningful programmes to be worked out to ensure progress and continuity.

And finally, *Tenth*, most of the exploited countries (virtually the whole of Africa) having been colonized, still suffer from the legacy of colonialism and have now moved into a neo-colonial stage in the whole imperialistic arrangement.

So, ten good reasons in my opinion, why Africa, like the rest of South, save Australia and New Zealand, is under-developing *rather* than developing. Of course, there are other powerful forces that make development in the exploited world an illusion at the moment, but this only serves to further complicate the whole situation.

EDUCATION SYSTEMS AS MAIN CONTRIBUTORY FACTORS TOWARDS UNDER-DEVELOPMENT IN AFRICA

Here, again because of colonialism and the legacy of it, the **wrong** type of education is in operation in the exploited world as we have seen above. It is limited in the sense that it only caters for urbanized type of life and not rural. It completely ignores the basic factors that may help sustain any growing nation in its bid for national development. It teaches the exploited world population to aspire to a First world type of life without providing for it.

It lays less emphasis on technical subjects and more on schools which only lead to urban white collar type of employment, thus allowing urban development while denying rural development.

Education is the means by which any society achieves growth and development. But it has to be the right kind of education and relevant to that society. It has to embody in it the culture and the aspirations of the people of that society. It has to be local both in taste and expression. It has, most importantly, to be geared towards the **development** and the **advancement** of that society.

All this is sadly lacking in the education systems on the continent of Africa. Therefore, education as such is not serving the interests of Africa, but those abroad. How on earth can education systems in Africa be helping to develop Africa when not one single scientific invention or manufactured product—manufactured by Africans is selling on the world market?

> Perhaps the greatest tragedy in all this, is the fact that the African buys everybody else's manufactured goods, hence develops other people's economies and not his own

I'll give you an example:
When we Africans go shopping for cars, home appliances, cameras, watches, TVs, radios, clothes, weapons—*especially* weapons, we are helping to develop and strengthen not Africa's economies as such, but those of the manufacturers! I want every African worth his salt to think seriously think about this.

> Moreover, all these products mentioned above are invariably manufactured out of raw materials from Africa

We are the only race in the world that has acquired the exclusive **privilege** of making everybody else rich except ourselves!

Here is another example of how the education system really doesn't help the African as it does not teach him how to manufacture things:

You see everytime an African buys one Peugeot car, easily ten Frenchmen are guaranteed a job and food in their stomach—the foreign currency used to purchase that car denies fifty Africans job opportunities. Everytime we go to buy weapons from wherever they are manufactured, millions of Africans go without jobs and food in their stomachs. Worse still, those weapons are used to *kill* Africans.

In other words, while we are creating jobs and wealth for the manufacturing countries, we are at the same time guaranteeing poverty and misery in Africa. The solution to all this being simply to manufacture these things ourselves and as well sell them on the world market. Pure and simple! Any African who believes that Africa is going to achieve economic independence without first industrializing her economies, needs to have his head examined fast!

> So, the so-called educated African for the most part is basically illiterate. He possesses proficiency certificates in English, French, and other such language and derives great personal pleasure in speaking them. But when it comes to things scientific and technological inventions, he remains unbashfully illiterate. Even greater the tragedy, he knows not the fact!

COLONIAL STRUCTURES AS CONTRIBUTING FACTORS TOWARDS UNDER-DEVELOPMENT

I come again to the question of colonialism as a phase that under-developed and **still** under-develops Africa. This third phase of exploitation might easily have been the most devastating for the continent of Africa. This was the milestone in the sad chapter of the colonization of Africa. During this period, the foundation for the exploitation of Africa was laid by Europe. The same instruments by which the colonizing forces used to exploit and **under-**developed the African are still in operation to this day. All that changed were faces and very little else!

Here, I'm aware that some explanation is necessary in order to adequately illustrate this point.

THE COLONIAL SET-UP

(a)   The set-up of the colonial structures was such that the little there was of development, only took place in urbanized areas.

(b)   That only few with access to urbanized life were better off economically; that meant of course the occupying forces, if the word should be used.

(c)   Full participation in this limited development and the fruits of it, had to be preceded by a Western, hence foreign type of education. This education had and still has to be paid for.

(d)   The administration structures created by the colonizing powers were based on their home systems hence foreign, to Africa with her unique culture.

(e)   The rest of the national population mainly resident in rural areas, was largely ignored and only used as tools for development that only benefited the urbanized and already better-off few.

Now, come to the so-called national independence and self-determination across Africa in the late fifties and early sixties, the same oppressive structures were left untouched and continued with.

A new African elite was created to replace the out-going colonial forces. Westminister, French, and American styles of government were quickly installed ostensibly to see to the administration of these new and emerging nations. The men who took over the administration would mainly have been educated in the capitals of the former colonizing nations. They would inevitably so, have a Western, hence foreign approach to local situations. They would see development through the eyes of the Westerner and not the home grown African. They would want to impress upon Africa a Western liberal-democracy, without the Western culture and values to accompany it. They would create national parliaments but not the institutions to cater for differences. In other words, they would transfer these systems of government, into Africa but would not live through the dictates of the very systems.

As I understand them, Western systems of government operate with separation of powers. The judiciary, legislature, and government exist as three entities within, each functioning as a consequence of the other, but neither institution possessing absolute power.

The judiciary, for example, may over-rule the government on a matter, much as the government can, through legislation, enact laws to contain the judiciary.

> This important separation of powers, is lacking in the way that African governments function

Therefore, these systems in Africa, have produced nothing but power-hungry dictators who have come to power and stayed on as if they were endowed with two male genitals! Is it any wonder that these systems have miserably failed and continue to do so?

It would be wrong to say that only the Western liberal-democracy variant has been tried in Africa. Other non-liberal variants have been tried, but equally failed miserably.

And then something resembling Jacques Rousseau's general will is being tried at the moment. Single party states have emerged purporting to represent the will of the majority. These systems, however, allow no room for opposition and have naturally created dissidents who can't go along with everybody.

Then the Communist variant has been tried with poor results due to lack of the necessary discipline. Then military dictatorships have failed miserably too. So Africa has had to contend with four different types of forces,

Inferior weapons sold to Africans at exorbitant prices. These weapons are useless in a conventional war, but capable of killing Africans

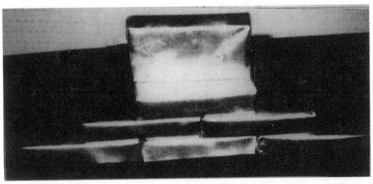

Yes, there is hope for Africa—the gold above is a fraction of his wealth. The problem is he doesn't control it and that is why he is 'poor'

No More Lies About Africa

each pulling in the opposite direction. There is first, the Western liberal democracy variant pulling in one direction; then the Communist in the other direction; then the military dictatorship in its own direction; and then the African, non-market capitalist and non-communist variant struggling to find expression. You obviously end up with chaos and nothing short of it. All due to colonialism and neo-colonialism as the advanced stage of imperialism.

IS THERE ANY HOPE FOR AFRICA?

Inevitably, the question has to be asked. The same question also pre-supposes that there is no hope at all at the moment. But as to whether there can be hope for a future Africa, a close examination of her potential and resources is necessary.

Yes, there can be hope for Africa. No continent is as best placed to forge on with meaningful development as Africa is. She, more than any other continent on earth, has all the necessary ingredients to make real development a reality, and not just a dream. She has the necessary mineral resources in *gold, copper, iron ore, uranium, diamond, bauxite, oil,* to name but a few, also rich and fertile soils, waters and the human resources for the miracle to be possible! The fertile soils that Africa is so blessed with, if properly exploited, could easily make her self-sufficient in food for decades and probably centuries to come.

Africa is the only continent on earth that need

not import anything from the outside world

The other grossly under-employed resources are the human resources. Masses are out of work in Africa, not because of **unemployment,** but because of **under-employment.** It is important to draw this distinction because being unemployed as the word is freely used in industrial countries implies that the employment sectors are overflowing with a trained manpower, mental and physical. Whereas being 'under-employed' as the term should apply to Africa and the exploited world as a whole, implies that there neither exist flourishing employment sectors, nor the necessary trained personnel to fill the sectors if created!

WHAT MUST HAPPEN BEFORE THE MIRACLE HAPPENS?

First, the African will have to go through a period of **mental** de-colonization, hence be mentally free and regain his African image and culture.

Second, the lost spirit of **nationalism** will have to be recaptured and rekindled as the driving force towards a national identity and development.

Third, the will and desire to be free and **self-reliant** will have to be more evident than has hitherto been the case.

Fourth, **visionary** leadership will have to re-assert itself to recapture the lost dynamism.

Fifth, **unity** of common purpose will have to prevail in order to combine all the resources for continental development. For example, we urgently need a common language as the colonial languages, e.g. French, English, Portuguese, and Spanish only continue to divide us.

> Can you imagine the might of Africa if she had one language, one government, one currency, one army and one people?

How about Kiswahili for a start? So far it's the single most international African language.

Sixth, **economic co-operation** will have to prevail to lessen dependence on outside non-profitable markets. Here, I'm talking about inter-trade between African countries.

Seventh, fraternal **co-existence** will have to be institutionalized in order to remove the state of war which exists at the moment and threatens to engulf the continent in an outright conflict.

Eighth, **freedoms** of the individual (to borrow the liberal democracy terminology) will have to be guaranteed in order to allow free expression, free movement, free association, hence enable full human development. Also, the kind of atmosphere to enable professional Africans to work in will have to be guaranteed. Today, Africa has lost most of her brain power to political instabilities. Lack of real economic development hasn't helped much either.

Ninth, systems left behind by colonial forces, will have to be **re-structured** in order that more congenial and African oriented systems of government can be created.

Tenth, **education** systems will have to be restructured to be more relevant to Africa and lay more emphasis on

Products such as these have not only strengthened the Japanese economy, but also earned Japan world respect—Africa take note!

industrial and **agricultural** development.

Eleventh, more emphasis will have to be laid on becoming **industrially** viable and economically independent, in order that political independence may have full meaning as hitherto it has not.

> In other words, we must stop exporting raw materials, and instead, export processed finished products, to be sold on world markets.

That is exactly where hope for Africa lies, in my considered opinion.

DISCRIMINATION BECAUSE OF ECONOMIC DEPENDENCY, BUT NOT COLOUR

The notion that peoples of African descent are discriminated against by whites, because of colour distinction is nonsensical. Discrimination by whites against blacks, is purely **economic.** That's to say, peoples of African descent encounter discrimination because of their collective economic dependence on the white world. But not just because they happen to be black!

Colour was, and is still used as the measuring yard stick, in order to disarm and as a result permanently disable the black man. As long as he believes that being black renders him an inferior species, he will forever have an inferior view of himself, hence do little to improve his grossly disadvantaged economic position. Never in the history of humankind has the pigment of one's skin, ever accurately determined the inner quality of man, let alone his intellectual potential. Never!

One hardly requires an economics degree from Harvard Business School to realize that as a race that only *consumes* but never **produces**, that race is vulnerable and ever at the tender mercies of producers.

In former so-called racist South Africa, the Japanese were classed as 'honorary whites' Why? Because Japan is a manufacturing giant.

Years ago, Michael Jackson, an African American, signed the world's richest contract in the history of advertising, $15 million dollars to do a half-minute commercial for the *Pepsi-Cola* Company. In the 1980's, the hottest TV show in America and believe it or not, in then apartheid South Africa as well, was not the all white *Dallas,* but the all African American *Cosby Show!* Yet barely twenty years ago, African Americans were struggling to get minor parts in movies. Here, it seems expediency is the name of the game. As long as the black man sells the product, so what if he is black? *Really!*

Is There Hope For the African Person Home or Abroad?

I started this chapter by establishing the fact that the African person, wherever he is, isn't free at all. We saw how the basic differences that exist between the African person in Africa, and the African person abroad don't amount to anything like real freedom at all for either. I then concluded that both are principally not free at the moment.

So where does hope for the African person home or abroad lie? One possible direction to follow would be the Garvey way.

Garvey, like no other known African leader, addressed himself to the plight of all African peoples of the world. He never disassociated one African situation from another. He firmly believed that until all are free, neither could claim real freedom. He tirelessly and unselfishly strove to see that the race had more sense of purpose about it; that the African person should sacrifice everything and seek to be self-reliant, creative, and inventive in order to attain real freedom and independence. For that, he was ostracized by both black and white alike!

So Garvey lived and played his humble part. He ultimately succeeded in awakening and inspiring the African person to fight for independence and self-dignity.

But somewhat, the zeal for the cause is no longer there. There is complacency about the African today. The old dynamism that saw him make an impression on the world scene immediately after last century's Second European War

seems to have all but evaporated. He now sits back immersed in the old dream that one day things will be better for him; that he is owed a living and protection by the white man; and that one day, the white man will wake up one morning feeling benevolent (and perhaps crazy), and say: "Here you are, black man; have my wealth; have my industry and technology!" What a dream world we live in! Wake up Africa! As per his conduct in Africa, the white man is too wicked to be trusted.

Hope lies exactly in the direction that Marcus Garvey wanted the African to go. Said he once: "The African will have to build his own government, industry, art, science, literature, and culture, before the world will stop to consider him. Until then, we are wards of a superior race and civilization, and the outcasts of a standard social system." He couldn't have been more right!

As we have seen above, the African today has no creation selling on world markets. He boasts neither car; nor plane; nor watch; nor radio; nor TV; nor pocket calculator; nor tractor; nor bicycle for that matter, or any form of machinery, invented and manufactured by him out of his raw materials, which incidentally, he has in abundance. The white man has to do it all for him. That is why he is so poor!

> To survive, he will have to recapture the old magic of his creative and inventive ancestors who saw to the birth of the world civilization and following in their brilliant foot-steps, restore lost glory.

That is where hope, might lie for the African person, home and in the diaspora.

10

Back To An African Identity

African Names

O ginga Odinga! Everyone, well almost everyone has heard of Jaramogi Oginga Odinga. He was Kenya's most colorful vice president.

One Sunday as a young man, he and his wife took their three sons to be baptized. The church was packed. The Reverend was an African brother.

Odinga carried the eldest of the boys on his shoulders to the alter for the ritual. The Reverend asked for the child's names;

"Oburu Amolo Odinga," Odinga proudly announced. The Reverend asked for the Christian names.

"Oburu Amolo," came the reply from Odinga.

"What!" Exclaimed the shocked Reverend.

"Oburu Amolo," repeated Odinga.

"How about his Christian names?" The Reverend insisted.

"Those are *his* Christian names!," Odinga shot back.

"But those are pagan names, Mr.Odinga!" The clergyman cried.

"Both Oburu and Amolo were great leaders of their people. They obeyed all God's laws. They offended no one. I'm naming my eldest son after them."

"Mr. Odinga, what is the second son's name?"

"Raila Odinga.!"

"What are his Christian names?"

"Raila Odinga!"

"Mr.Odinga, if you do not have proper Christian names such as Edward, George, Robert, and so on, I'm not going to baptize your sons."

"And if you are not going to baptize my sons with those illustrious names I gave you, then you will not baptize them with English names you call Christian, either."

Odinga and his wife were unceremoniously thrown out of the church. Here was an African, unable to name his children African names, in Africa, by an African priest!

Odinga being Odinga, eventually got his way and had his children named African names. But not before being humiliated for wanting to hold on to his African identity!

Now listen to me carefully, my brothers and sisters. Now is the time to get rid of these offensive names. Why? Because they are not **African**!

Has it ever occurred to you that we are the only people in the world without a true identity? You can tell a Chinese, a Russian, an Indian, miles away—because of identity.

If I were to tell you that a Mr. Yu Pin Ho was coming to see me, you would have no difficulty assuming that Mr. Yu Pin Ho was from Shanghai, would you?

But contrast the above with me telling you that Richard was coming to have dinner with me. You would not automatically assume that Richard was from England, because the name Richard is used by Europeans and converted Africans alike.

There is probably nothing wrong with these so-called Christian names as such. The problem I find with them, however, is that they deny us our true identity. They constantly remind us of the lie that we were **nothing** until the white man came and converted us to his ways. That is my basic quarrel with them. I'm constantly asking myself: Where is the African's identity? He speaks everyone else's languages; he wears everyone else's clothes; has assumed everyone else's culture; he bears everyone else's names; he aspires to everyone else's way of living; he eats everyone else's food and as we saw in the previous chapter; he buys everyone else's products!

*   *   *

I realize that by now I have upset a lot of people. But the truth had to be told in the end. For this reason, I offer apologies to no one!

Now is the time to think in terms of a true identity—an African identity. I beg you (on my knees), and in the names of Ruwenzori and Kilimanjaro, to get rid of these offensive names and assume your **true,** rich African names.

Here are some of them:

GAMBIA

Names	Pronunciation	Meaning
Male		
Alieu	A-liu	
Abdoulie	Abdoulai	
Baboucarr	Bab-uucar	
Omar	Oma	
Ousman	Osi-man	
Edrissa	Edirissa	
Musa	M-usa	
Bakari	Bakari	
Saihou	Sayihu	
Tamsir	Tamisi	
Demba	De-mba	
Kebba	Kebba	
Onusainou	Osayinu	
Female		
Fatoumatta	Fatumata	
Aminatta	Amina-tta	
Sainabou	Sai-nabu	
Ashiatou	Ashiituu	
Mariama	Maria-ma	
Safiatou	Safia-tuu	
Ramatulie	Ramatulii	

Kordou	Koduu
Awa	A-wa
Olimatta	Oli-ma-tta
Sira	Sii-ra
Maimuna	Ma-yimuna
Nyima	Nyi-ma
Oumie	U-mii

IVORY COAST

Male

Kouakou	Kwa-kuu
Koffi	Ko-ffii
Yao	Yawo
Kragbe	Kra-bii
Kipre	Ki-rrii
Lago	Laago
Santigie	Sa-ntigyi
Sorie	Sorri
Brima	Bri-maa
Ibrahim	Ibrahiim
Sheku	She-kuu
Lamina	La-minaa
Idrissa	Edirissa

Female

Akissi	Aki-ssi
Adjoua	Ajwa
Amena	Ameena

Ahoua	Awuwa
Aya	Ayaa
Affoue	Afuwii
Amoin	Amwani
Nana	Na-na
Adenike	Ade-nike
Aikoula	Ayikuula
Binta	Bi-nta
Ndidi	Ndi-di
Isa	Ayisa
Olatunde	Olantuunde

KENYA

Male

Kenyatta	Kin-yatta	Maasai Belt
Mwamburi	Mwa-mburii	He that owns goat
Mwang'ombe	Mwa-ng'ombe	Owns cattle
Mwakio	Mwa-kio	Born at night
Mwachia	Mwaki-ya	Born on the way
Mwavua	Mwa-vuwa	Born during rainy season
Mwadime	Mwa-dime	Born early in the morning.
Mwakwari	Mwa-kwari	Born during cold season
Mwacharo	Mwa-cyaro	He who must

		travels
Muturi	Mu-turii	Blacksmith
Muchoki	Mu-kyoki	Born to replace the dead
Muriithi	Mu-rithi	Who looks after cattle
Macharia	Ma-chriya	Who looks for wealth
Kioko	Kiyoko	Born in the morning
Mutuku	Mu-tuku	Born at night
Mutuso	Mu-tiso	The shining one
Kilonzo	Ki-lonzo	Made too much noise at birth

Female

Njoki	Njo-ki	Returned from the dead
Nyakio	Nya-kiyo	Hard working woman
Kalekye	Kal-kyee	Born without pain
Nyambura	Nya-mbura	Born during rainy season
Akinyi	Aki-nyi	Born in the morning
Atieno	Atyeno	Born at night
Anyango	Any-n	Born in the afternoon
Akello	Ake-llo	Gift from God
Alouch	Aluwokyi	Spring
Awiti	A-witi	Survivor
Apiyo	A-piyo	Girl twin

NIGERIA

Male

Ifeanyichukwa	Ifanyi-kyukwa	All possible with God
Onyemaaechi	Onye-makyi	Nobody can predict tomorrow
Chukwumaechi	Kyu-ku-makyi	Only God can predict tomorrow
Ezechukwu	Eze-kyu-kuu	King chosen by God
Udo	U-do	Peace
Ngozi	Ngo-zi	Blessing
Nkechi	Kepkyi	God's gift
Ogechi	Oge-kyi	God's time
Kelechi	Ke-lekyi	Thanks to God
Nkemdilim	Nke-ndilimi	Let all that is mine remain
Chinedum	Kyi-nedamu	God leads me
Chibueze	Kyi-buweze	God is King
Obiagiliaku	Obya-gilyaku	The bride has come to enjoy the wealth of the bridegroom's family
Ndubuisi	Nduwi-si	Life comes first

SOMALIA

Male

Ashkir	Ash-kir	Brown
Bulbul	Balibu	Fussy
Farah	Fa-rah	Joy

Gadid	Ga-diid	Midday
Hibe	Hi-be	Excellent
Ismail	Ism-ayili	
Kulmiye	Kulumiye	He that unties
Liban	Lib-ana	Blessed

Female

Hur	Huwa	Light
Qorah	Qoraha	Sunny
Samatar	Samata	Blessed
Tonyar	To-yar	Slim
Waberi	Wa-be-rii	Dawn
Ulusow	Oluso	Heavy

SWAZILAND

Male

Mfayana	Fananya	Little boy
Vusumzi	Vusunzi	
Mandlenkosi	Madilikosi	
Mpini	P-ini	
Sipho	Sifo	A gift
Majaheni	Majeheni	
Mhlangano	Miliangano	Meeting
Velebatfu	Velebafuu	
Velaphi	Velafii	We come from over seas
Phesheya	Fisheya	

Mfanuzile	Fanuzile	
Bonginkosi	Bongi-kosi	Praise the king
Bafana	Ba-fana	Boys

Female

Bhekimpi	Bekimpi	
Thokozile	Zokozi-le	Happiness
Sibongile	Sibonge-le	Thankful
Nomsa	No-sa	Kindness
Ntombi	Nto-mbi	A Girl
Lomgcibelo	Logisibe-lo	Born Saturday
Lomsotfo	Lo-maso-fo	Born Sunday
Lomsombuluko	Loso-mbulu-ko	Born Monday
Dimisile	Dimisi-le	

ZIMBABWE

Male

Tafirinyika	Ta-fe-renee-ka	We die for our country
Takura	Ta-koo-rah	We have come of age
Chengetai	Cha-nga-taye	Preserve
Mutsa	Mu-u-tza	Mercy
Simba	Seem-mba	Power
Tafara	Ta-fah-rah	We are happy
Ngoni	Ngo-ni	Mercy
Tamuka	Ta-mu-kah	We are awake
Kudzai	Kuz-ai	Give thanks to
Fungai	Fungai	Think

Female

Rudo	Roo-doh	Love
Chipo	Chee-poh	Gift
Tendai	Te-nda-yi	Praise
Chiedza	Kyi-nza	Special
Thandiwa	Tandi-wa	Be loved
Ruwa	Roo-wah	Flower
Nyarai	Nya-rah-hi	Respect
Nomusa	No-mu-sah	Mercy
Sitembile	Si-te-mbile	Trust
Sibongile	Si-bo-ngile	Thanks

An Epilogue

Dear Reader,

I hope that you are better educated about Africa now.
If there's anything you wish to share with me, don't hesitate
to write to me through my publishers:

Mungu Ibariki Afrika! (God Bless Africa!)

Index